The Journal of the Man

Some trust in chariots and some in horses,
But we trust in the name of the Lord our God.

Psalm 20: 7

Copyright © 2007 Thomas Lile
All rights reserved.
ISBN: 1-4196-3066-0
ISBN-13: 978-1419630668

www.CreateSpace.com/3140429

THOMAS LILE

EDITED BY BARBARA FORSHAG

THE JOURNAL OF THE MAN

2007

The Journal of the Man

> I have put my words in your mouth
> and covered you with the
> shadow of my hand.
>
> Isaiah 51: 16

*The Words Recorded Here Are Dedicated To Susan Jones,
My Wonderful Sister, Who Suffered With
Me Through A Childhood Not Of Our Choosing.
And Who, Having Come Into The Knowledge Of The Truth,
Spared Nothing To Reach Back And Grab The Hand Of A
Younger Brother.*

Enlighten the people generally, and
Tyranny and oppressions of body and
Mind will vanish like evil spirits at
The dawn of day.

Thomas Jefferson
1816

I remember that warm April afternoon just as though it was yesterday. I was just a young boy, eager to see life as it really was and foolish enough to think it was mine for the taking.

Jumping from the back seat of the Chevy, I dashed into the little brick house on Forest Park Road and bolted through the door into mother's bedroom. The room reeked of urine, and a trail of bright red vomit led my eyes toward the unlit bathroom. Her body was frozen there, sunk over the toilet seat, the head hanging downward into the wastebasket alongside. Unable to speak, I stood there frozen in place. The foul odor engulfed the room, and I inched backward out the door and ran away.

Daddy had died in this same room only four years earlier…and now mom. How could these terrible things have ever happened? We were not evil people; I was not a bad son. I wondered if the nightmare would ever end.

Having to stand idly by and watch both your mother and father slowly drink themselves to death will tear at the very fabric of the mind. It is an agony for which there can be little comparison, echoing through every day and distorting each event in life. The personal pain of a young boy who must return home each evening to an environment of indictment and hate gradually eats away at the heart. Over time one prefers to simply stay away, to run toward the highest mountain or become lost in the darkest cave.

Mother's funeral was a simple gathering as family and friends gathered under the quiet, shady oaks in a New Orleans cemetery. The beautiful mahogany box bearing her remains had been transferred from our home in Florida to Louisiana in the baggage car of a passenger train, a train that slowly wound its way through the night along the Gulf Coast. Of necessity, I sat alone among the other passengers that night, accompanying her lifeless body to its final destination. I was a small boy, abandoned by all, forced by events around me to know more than he should really know. I wondered what now would become of me.

The year was 1964, and I found myself parentless, an orphan. In truth, perhaps, I had actually been without real parents for most of my life. Never having been a part of a real family, I spent much time observing others, trying to comprehend how things really were supposed to be. It was unfortunate that no adults around me were willing to step forward to show the way, and I languished in the sorrow of it all.

In the months and years that followed, I desperately needed to come to terms with the painful past. It was an innocent mistake, to believe that all those years of torment would simply be swept away in the riptide of my parents passing. The uncomfortable truth was that the sins of the father would be visited upon the son, and I could not have foreseen the days of misfortune coming my way.

* * * * *

I fell in love and married in 1972. It was a sharp, clear day, near Christmas as I recall, and my pursuit of real happiness seemed to be right on course. Throughout my entire boyhood, I had earnestly sought the love so lacking from a close tie with mom and dad. And so, on my wedding day, I was more than confident that my life-long search to fill the void in my heart had come to a wonderful end with the "joining of this man and this woman." Very young and very naïve, I believed that no matter what happened, our love would overcome all. I guess I thought my wife felt the same way. In the years that would follow, this naïve young man would become older and wiser and come to understand that most people have what I have dubbed the "drop-out point." For some, the "drop-out point" may come early; for others it may appear later. It is that time when, in any relationship, the situation becomes intolerable for one of the players, turning the happiest day in one's life into the saddest. On that day vows are broken, exaggerations become commonplace, and demons are made of those who walked upright and faithful lives.

There can be little doubt that I, having few good role models to draw upon, was hardly a great husband. However, there had been planted a deep reservoir of heart within me, manifested in an unflinching, maddening determination to never quit, to never walk away until the conflict had dissipated. As my wife was packing to leave me, she said, "You never share with me from the deepest part of your heart, and you never do anything to show you care for me." I winced at hearing her litany of grievances, but there could be no doubt that I had earned the withering critique. So, alone again, I made a promise to myself to change my way of doing things, a down payment on things to come.

For many of us who have not known marriage to be the great "joy" we had anticipated, it is truly difficult to write or even discuss the subject in this day and time. For most men and women, the mere word "marriage" conjures up the greatest hopes and, at the same time, the greatest disappointments of their lives. Rampant divorce has ripped apart the very concept of "one love for one lifetime." Sadly, even people in the Christian faith now fill the dockets of local courts, demanding their piece of man's justice while, at the very same moment, praying frantically that their God will not execute *His* justice upon them! The result is a community of broken people coming from every walk of life. These individuals are the walking wounded, the injured for whom there is no sick bed or nurse, the true and the faithful for whom almost all have turned away.

* * * * *

In the early 1970's, while working as tennis professional at a resort on the Florida coast, I made the acquaintance of Christopher Gilman. Chris Gilman was a New York millionaire whose family owned the largest privately held paper company in the United States. Gilman would often fly his family and friends from New York to his estate on the St. Mary's River which separated Florida from Georgia. I was among the invited guests at his White Oak Plantation on numerous occasions, hitting tennis balls with business associates and family members.

One day, on the ride north from Jacksonville to the Gilman Plantation, I festered over my situation at home. My marriage was falling apart, my job strangling me, and I was unsure of what to do next. My thoughts wandered to the man called Jesus, of whom my sister had spoken so often. Did He actually exist? I decided to ask out loud, "If you're really out there, would you show yourself to me?" There was an eerie silence. What happened next, I could never fully explain. In the blink of an eye, I became aware of the presence of someone else in the car with me. I was no longer alone. I drove on for the next hour in a state of raw ecstasy, feeling as though the blinders had been abruptly snatched from my eyes.

In the days that followed, I was insane. I read every book that I could find that spoke of this man named Jesus. In a matter of days the Savior would move, for me, off the pages of historical literature and begin to reshape the direction of all I undertook. Over the next few months, my wife and I joined a local congregation and laid ourselves at the feet of those in authority over us in the church. However, I was slow to catch on, and over time my passion for spiritual things began to cool.

Six years slipped away after my "Damascus Road" experience. It was 1980, when my wife, my four year-old daughter, and I moved into a small bungalow near the beach. Things seemed pleasant enough, and we had the usual struggles of a young family. Little did I know that the hammer was about to fall.

My wife had left for a ten-day business trip to North Carolina, and I was, as always, entranced by my sweet daughter as she skipped happily about the yard. Returning at week's end, my wife seemed troubled. She avoided talking, left suddenly, and stayed away into the next morning. Days later, her confession came…she had been having an affair with her boss for months and wanted, even then, to be with him. I was destroyed. She packed some things and left the house, leaving me to feed and care for our small daughter. Each night I sat alone crying in the darkness wishing that the Lord would take me away and be done with it. Over the next few weeks, I experienced a pain so deep into the very core of my being that I have not fully recovered from it even to this day. In the months that followed, I was asked to leave and served with papers of divorce.

Denied the custody of my only daughter and forced from my home, I asked myself where the wonderful God who had revealed His face so gently to me could be? Alone once again, I sat in a small efficiency sorting out the twisted pieces of what remained of my life. There was no doubt that throughout my youth I had sought love in all the wrong places—in the clubs, in the arms of strange women, and in the deeds of life. It was then that I found myself on my face pleading with the Lord to appear once again, just as He had done years before on the road to Gilman Plantation. I desperately needed to touch Him, to see Him, to know again the power of His resurrection. Kneeling by the bed, through a downpouring of tears, I came face to face with real love…on the bloodied face and in the piercing eyes of the carpenter from Nazareth. Never, until that night, had I comprehended the completeness of His love for me, and I knew then that nothing would ever again be the same.

* * * * *

OCTOBER 12, 1981

It is today that I begin the journal. It is, in truth, a selfish project. I sit here alone in the dim light, caring very much that my daughter will someday know the whole story. I also care that those people whose paths I will cross in the years to come will know what really happened. It is important that my thoughts, although surely just my own, be considered in the total body of my life's work. In no way do I underestimate the vastness of this undertaking. To go back and purge the memory of its poisons is much like seeking a valued pearl in the garbage.

Perhaps my real motive is to engage in the healing of emotions and the thought of this seems strange and somewhat ironic. After having lived many years, I have spent more time healing from life than actually living it. I am not afraid to die; I am afraid, however, that I may never get a chance to live.

> Consider it pure joy, my brothers, whenever you face trials of many kinds, because you know that the testing of your faith develops perseverance. Perseverance must finish it's work so that you may be mature and complete, and lacking nothing.
>
> James 1: 2, 3, 4

DECEMBER 19, 1981

Much as the legendary seer Nostradamus was known to peer off into the future, I often catch my thoughts reeling backwards. I feel as if I am able to see the past so clearly. Childhood, a time of laughing and foolishness for many, was not that for me. Instead, my days were full of chaos and shame while the solitary nights were cold, ruthless wanderings into fear.

I remember those evenings well. My bed sheets became the armor of the timid knight they encircled as I huddled there in the darkness, wide eyed, clenching the side of the mattress. I wanted so often to summon up the courage to run away, but I had no place to go. Every minute became an hour while I prayed silently that I would not become the focus of my parents' attention. Screams, yells, threats, and all manner of verbal abuse were launched and returned, then faded away to be co-mingled with murky dreams. I ached for soft hands and tender words from my mother who was able to supply neither. Many times I had so hoped that a hero would suddenly appear coming down the hallway, and that I would be snatched away from this torment and taken to a place of safety and calm. But no one ever came.

Riding my bike home each evening, I would excitedly steal a glance into the lighted windows that passed along the way, trying to get a glimpse of the people inside. I often wondered if they, like I, lived a life of dread. In the years since those childhood days, I have heard the revulsion of others…how some were beaten and chained to basement stairs, and others were forced to endure hardships and degrading behavior too painful to describe. Nothing of such an extreme physical nature was done to me. No, my torture was simply that I did not exist. Often told by my mother that I was "not wanted," I gritted my teeth and determined in my own mind that I must go on. Over time, I arrived at the knowledge that I had come "through" her but not "from" her….for the hero I had sought for so long finally did appear. He was there before me; His words piercing the history of time and space calling for me to come. His eyes would not leave me while His lips uttered the sounds I had always yearned to hear. And that night, when the hero finally came down the hallway, I came face to face with Jesus Christ the Lord.

> Yea, though I walk through the valley of the shadow of death, I will fear no evil; for thou art with me, thy rod and thy staff they comfort me. Thou preparest a table before me in the presence of mine enemies; thou anointest my head with oil; and my cup runneth over…..
> Surely goodness and mercy shall follow me all the days of my life; and I will dwell in the house of the Lord forever.
>
> Psalm 23: 3, 4, 5, 6

JANUARY 4, 1982

When I was a boy, sharing family "secrets" just wasn't the thing to do. Anyway, who would want to reveal that their parents, both of them, were drunks? Dad was born in 1906, into a small farming community in northern Alabama. The family lived in a modest home set up on a hill away from the highway, surrounded by rolling meadows dancing in clover as far as the eye could see. His parents were people of the earth, and he knew no life other than the quiet hometown that knew them all well. In 1925, his father enrolled him as a freshman at Alabama's proud institution of higher learning, *Auburn University*. There he wowed them at everything and graduated with honors in 1928 in electrical engineering. He was a proud inductee into Phi Delta Theta, and in his final months of college, his peers chose him to be the most representative member of the senior class. Unsure of what to do next, he traveled in May of that year to the Theological Seminary at Alexandria, Virginia, where he spent a week as an observer, considering a role for himself in the ministry. To the outsider he stood a gorgeous man, black hair pulled close to the head (as was the style in those days) with impeccable good looks that would rival any movie star. So, in the summer of 1928, the man who never suffered from a deficit of doubt had achieved almost everything any one would want. The world was his and he could do with it whatever his heart desired. Daddy went on to marry and have two children, a daughter and then a son. Life began to take its toll on him and the man from Alabama, who had once considered taking up the cross as his life's work, decided it was not as practical as it had once seemed. His indifference to his own family's well-being was breathtaking. He began to drink, just a few at the beginning, until he could no longer do without.

At age 54, thirty-two years after he stood at the pinnacle of life's success, daddy lay dying of alcoholism is his own bed, his hands trembling as he drew his final, difficult breath. He had told me many times that he knew no good reason for why I was even here, and the words "I love you" had never escaped his lips. There was no way any of us could have known the price we would be compelled to pay for the choices he had made. I was always grappling to explain the almost incalculable betrayal of our family for which he was responsible and considered it all a tragedy that only time would come to heal. Father never got a chance to gaze into the faces of his own beautiful grandchildren. His college friends were now gone; he was all alone. His wife despised him, his daughter feared him, and his son…well, his son never even knew who he was.

> Therefore, since we are surrounded by such a great cloud of witnesses, let us throw off everything that hinders and the sin that so easily entangles, and let us run with perseverance the race marked out for us.
>
> Hebrews 12: 1

JANUARY 19, 1982

Four years elapsed between the sudden death of my father in April 1960 and the discovery of my mother dead in her bathroom in April of 1964. In that interlude, I was an eyewitness to the certainty that there was a "hell" because I lived in it. Mother was not coherent for two consecutive days, cloistered away in her bedroom for hours on end and eventually falling asleep mired in her own vomit. Distraught and unstable, she would awaken and roam the hallways of our house after midnight shouting obscenities at me and waving a huge butcher knife she had removed from the kitchen. There were many nights when I feared she would, in a drunken stupor, take my life. One of her favorite tricks was to take all the fuses out of the fusebox, hiding them so well even *she* could not recall their whereabouts. As a result, we would go for days without the ability to run the electricity in the overwhelming heat of one hundred degree Florida summers. I agonized over what to do, but as in so many phases of life, desperation brought no one to my side. As the year of 1964 began, I knew the torture could not go on much longer. By this time, mother's skin had turned a pasty yellow, and she could not bring herself to even glance into the mirror. Her hollow stare showed the years of self-inflicted abuse. Then it all ended. I cried.

Both of my parents died young and much too soon as their internal organs were virtually eaten away by relentless consumption of alcohol. These tragic events took place almost twenty summers ago but have left an indelible mark on those of us who were dutifully bound to be witnesses to those years of cruel exploitation. Living with them both, day after day, changed my way of seeing everything which is not all bad. After all, is not much of life deciding what you do and do *not* want to be? I am ever aware of the complete devastation alcohol has visited on my family dating back two generations. It is like a serpent, dangling the keys of pleasure before the unsuspecting, only to exchange them at the last moment for a push into eternal darkness. I have decided and committed myself to it....

The destructive legacy of my family must not be allowed to continue. It has fallen to me to break the yoke of bondage that has sent my fathers to an early grave.

> And be not conformed to this world: but be ye transformed by the renewing of your mind, that ye may prove what is that good, and acceptable, and perfect will of God.
>
> Romans 12: 2

MARCH 11, 1982

I was not the only young person terrorized by my father and mother. My sister Susan was four years older but no less a target of their spiraling insanity. She made it common practice to spend the night with girlfriends and rarely invited classmates over to our house. Mother, being the chameleon-like person she was, would torment her with accusations and physical threats, making a normally fragile relationship virtually impossible. Daddy's icy selfishness was immune to rational persuasion; so Susan and I tried valiantly to hide our shattered home life from our friends. Both of us instinctively understood that the price of our survival hung precariously on an unspoken fealty to silence and the punishment for talking out of school was a bridge we never wanted to cross. I would often need to think twice before saying nothing. We worried that the pall of fear over us would become common knowledge, and it would be revealed that the adults who lived there were completely dysfunctional. Even now, the tentacles of those years spent there threaten to ensnare us both as our memories are seared with the events of those awful days when hell was in session.

In 1959, Susan married her high school sweetheart, Lloyd Jones, and together they went on to have three beautiful daughters. Lloyd was later called into the ministry and today serves as a Baptist minister. They both tell the story of how, in the early days of their own ministry, they would enter my name on their prayer list and place it on the refrigerator door. The name remained there through many winters and many falls until one day, the ever-faithful Father, rolled away the stone from around my heart.

There will always be believers like Susan and Lloyd, the intercessors who serve with no fanfare and whose names will never appear on marquee lights. They are the foot soldiers who daily wage the war in the spiritual realm for the hearts and souls of men. They are the true heroes in a world that never even knew their names.

> But you are a chosen people, a royal priesthood,
> a holy nation, a people belonging to God.

That you may declare the praises of Him who
called you out of darkness
into His wonderful light.

1 Peter 2: 9

SEPTEMBER 4, 1982

There is no possible way I could tell you how many hours I have sat alone wondering why life has not worked out the way I had always envisioned it. In the innocence of youth, I had dreamed of caring parents, a boyhood cram-packed with fun and laughter, all the food I could eat, and a comfortable place to escape the world.

Instead, I was non-existent in the eyes of my mom and dad, had little to eat, and spent mealtime scouring for food in roach-infested cupboards. Of course, from the eyes of an adult, things look very different. If all my dreams had come to pass, I would not be the person that I, in truth, have come to be. It is within the possibility of reason that I could have become spoiled, adopted the nature of a bully, and have now no passion for the small wonders of life. Instead, I hopefully have emerged from brokenness as a new creation, a lover of simple truths, and sealed into a never-ending bond with the Giver of all life!

Who then can say that "bad" things are truly bad? Perhaps, they are merely the doors through which we pass on the painful road to fullness of spirit, and overcoming adversity may become the medicine that, once taken, heals the broken heart.

> God is our refuge and strength, a very present help in trouble. Therefore we will not fear, though the earth be removed and though the mountains be carried into the midst of the sea.
>
> Psalms 46: 1, 2

APRIL 20, 1983

Somewhere in the past I have heard the word "hard-heartedness" in common use. But this was different. Now it had taken on a human form, a face, a person to whom I had been married for almost a decade, the mother of my daughter. When I looked deep into her eyes, there was nothing there. It was like a blank wall, a fortress that I could neither reach nor climb. It was really frightening to see a real human being turned into a heart of stone. Like a giant boulder, her heart would simply not budge. It still sends cold shivers up my spine to think of it.

In the days and weeks since that horrible event, I have been abruptly wakened, panic struck, from the deepest sleep. My mind has continually relived the deep anguish of seeing my lovely young wife running to the outstretched arms of another. To deepen my desolation, my sweet daughter has become entangled in the web of her parents' making. It has become, for me, a living horror story…losing my only child into a judicial system that proclaims to "care" but has not the capacity or the moral will to seek the truth. Now, I finally understand why "justice" is portrayed as a blindfolded woman. These hauntings mold my thinking day after day until a siege mentality gradually settles into place. I have vowed to never rest until my daughter, now a virtual hostage in her own mother's home, can choose her own deliverance. Then and only then will I be able to close my eyes and receive the blessed peace of sleep. Please come, sweet sleep, for my own flesh and blood has been stolen away in the night, and the man in the black robe cares not.

> But God said to him, "You fool! This very night
> your life will be demanded from you. Then who
> will get what you have prepared for yourself?
> This is how it will be with anyone who stores up
> things for himself but is not rich toward God".

Luke 12: 20, 21

JULY 16, 1983

After having lived with my family for so long and then finding myself suddenly alone, my emotions flew in many different directions. Sometimes I enjoyed being alone, and at other times I thought the walls were about to crush me. I knew my healing awaited me in Paradise, but I am here now and must breathe another day. There were more than a few who came alongside, speaking words of love and adoration. But even they eventually fell away, seduced by the glamour of this world and the glitter of thirty pieces of silver.

At any rate, I needed a defense against such an occurrence ever taking place again. I decided I would become completely independent of everyone, asking for nothing, needing nothing, completely self-reliant. I could then be the master of my own fate, the ruler of my own world. Never again could I be denied anything; I would be complete right here, right now.

I should have known the whole thing was a house of cards. Indeed, the whole idea was foolishness. The man who wrote *No Man is an Island* was right. Knowing people, co-mingling your life with other people, assures great pain. However, it also holds the promise of tremendous rewards. May we learn to accept all, just as they are, with scars and blemishes just like our own. And may we come to trust others, knowing that occasionally a rose will bloom in the desert.

> Therefore, there is now no condemnation for those who are in Christ Jesus, because through Christ Jesus the law of the Spirit of life set me free from the law of sin and death.

Romans 8: 1, 2

JANUARY 26, 1984

An open letter to the wife who departed...
At the start, it was only the two of us. There was no hate, and my love for you knew no boundaries. When you parted, my love remained, but the recipient had now died. So I took that love, that devotion, and directed it to our daughter; she is now the center of my world. I know I was not the perfect husband; I know I made mistakes too many to count, which are now sadly branded upon your heart. But you should not have left; the King of Glory was still at work in me. Years have passed since that day. You are content with those days and see them merely as rain drops upon the window, but I cannot. I will always know the truth. Our daughter is a wonderful, beautiful little girl. So let her lesson be that her parents were flawed people, and let her life show the direction and purpose that ours did not. And when the last breath comes for you and me, let it be known that I would never walk away from those whom God has given to me. For marriage is not so much about happiness as it is holiness.

"For richer or for poorer...for better or for worse," which of these cherished words did you not understand? Or, like most, did you deem these vows as mere splashes of remembrances, not worthy to be valued as the days moved on?

To those of you who will come this way...remember that commitment can do what love cannot.

If you are a husband, I pray that you will be of sterner stuff and true to your wife and children. For God in Heaven will look down and meet your needs. If you are so fortunate as to become a father, live your life so as to be worthy of your children's respect. If you are single, seemingly alone, know that the angels of the Lord encamp around all those who truly love Him. No weapon formed against you shall prosper and every tongue that shall rise against you will be condemned. For this is the heritage of the servants of the Lord!

For our struggle is not against flesh and blood, but against the authorities, against the powers of this dark world and against the spiritual forces of evil in the heavenly realms.

Ephesians 6: 12

MARCH 1, 1984

It is beyond my grasp how any man or woman could walk away from vows proudly pronounced before a gathering of friends and witnessed by the hosts of heaven. How could that happen? Perhaps, there is needed only one word to make the impossible possible. The word is "selfishness". So I ask, "How many have deluded themselves into believing that *their* will is also the will of the Lord?" How can it be that the followers of the Christ speak of being "United with God" when they, in fact, cannot remain united with each other? For the church is splintered by infighting, with each faction hurling insults at the other, all claiming doctrinal superiority. And Christians are so interested in themselves that unbelievers can no longer see Christ in them. It is strange that some run so fast toward new truth when they cannot be obedient to the truth already possessed. We live in a world of counterfeits who seek the principles instead of the Prince, who have fallen in love with the creation instead of the Creator. And some, with noble intentions, speak of taking the gospel to the *third* world, but have yet to speak with that fellow in the *third* row. Perhaps before we can share the truth with others, we should stop lying to ourselves.

Marriage is, in truth, not for everyone. It is an honorable position that can only be entered into by honorable people. It demands integrity, responsibility, and keeping your promises in the face of overwhelming temptation. It is so unique that it should not be entered into by those who have no intrinsic sense of esteem for the majesty of it all. It is this deep abiding passion to go on that keeps the vows close to the heart. For if only one word could remain in the language, let it be the most significant, the one with the most potential. Let the one remaining word be *others*.

> In the world ye shall have tribulation: but be of good cheer;
> I have overcome the world.

John 16: 33

MAY 5, 1985

I dreamed big dreams as a teenager. I imagined for myself a marriage in Camelot with picket fences surrounding the rolling estate. I was sure of many close friends who would be there to catch me if I fell. But it didn't work out that way.

So, I put together a support system of my own devising. It was made up of allies who had not rushed for the exits, relatives, some believers, and a generous supply of others. These "others" were those whom Christ has not, to this date, yet called into His Kingdom. Ironically, it was this last group, "the yet uncalled", who were the least condemning, the most accepting, and the ones with whom I could most easily be myself. For I live in a world that does not know me, where vile, ignorant men call evil good and good is condemned as evil. For if the Lord gave us dominion over the birds of the air and the fish of the sea, how was it that so many became slaves to food and drink? And why do some scour the universe seeking signs of life.....while others finally find life in the womb and seek to destroy it? And I, the recipient of grace upon grace, shall walk with you beside every quiet brook and watch for you over every glorious horizon.

> Then God said "Let us make man in our image, after our likeness, and let them have dominion over the fish of the sea and over the birds of the air, and over the cattle, and over every creeping thing that creeps upon the earth".
>
> Genesis 1: 26

JUNE 1, 1985

I have often heard the comment "The Christian Army is the only army in the world that buries its own wounded." It is a sad truth but a truth no less. For some time I had worshipped among them. I sat in the pew day after day beside them as a brother in pursuit of the Truth. They had seen me, watched me, knew me, and yet that changed nothing. How quickly, once I was accused, did they, like Pilate, dip their hands in the basin, turn and walk away.

There was one notable exception. A man named David expressed great concern for me and the situation in which I found myself. A Messianic Jew, David called me faithfully every morning, praying, encouraging, and urging me to stay the course. As with the "David" of scriptures, he asked that I step forward and slay the giants who stood directly in sight. Looking back now, David was right. Thank you friend, wherever you may be.

> Greater love hath no man than this,
> that a man lay down his life for his friends.

John 15: 13

SEPTEMBER 11, 1985

Last month, I took a telephone call late in the evening from the office of the mayor. His assistant on the other end of the line informed me that the mayor had been converted to Christ last winter while attending a church service as part of his official function. As a result of this wonderful experience, the mayor's office now held a prayer luncheon once a month in a downtown hotel. I was asked to appear before the group assembled to testify to the reality of the living Christ. I thought it odd that I had been summoned by those I did not know when many I *did* know had quietly avoided me at all cost. On the day of the luncheon, my queasiness about public speaking was surely apparent to all as I entered the hall to see perhaps five hundred figures wearing starched ties and newly pressed business suits. Obviously, I had underestimated the number who worked in the downtown area and called themselves believers. There I stood, a run of the mill looking kid, clad in shorts and T-shirt, staring out at the assembly of finely dressed business leaders. Not a confident speaker, I swallowed hard while gazing out over the sea of faces that were turned my way. I shall never forget that day. They all looked at me with eyes of such great expectation. I wondered if they would believe a word I had to say.

That day I spoke the truth as I had lived and remembered it. I confessed my obvious failings, having spent the greatest part of my youth seeking love everywhere and finally discovering it in the beautiful eyes of the carpenter from Nazareth. When finished, I shook several hands and left knowing that I had spoken the words the Prince had always given me. Confident of that fact, I was satisfied that His will would be done in the individual lives of these fine men.

> Let the word of Christ dwell in you richly as you teach and admonish one another with all wisdom, and as you sing psalms, hymns and spiritual songs with gratitude in your hearts

to God. And whatever you do, whether in word or deed, do it all in the name of the Lord Jesus, giving thanks to God the Father through him.

Colossians 3: 16, 17

MARCH 8, 1986

Ever since the divorce, my daughter and I have worked hard at maintaining our closeness. I am more of a child than she so, when together, we often head for the pizza parlor to see the Big Bear Jamboree. But still, it isn't enough for me. I will accept the job for now, but never will I be satisfied with it.

Over the last few years, I have developed a relationship with an ex-college basketball star who has come to my aid in difficult times. This great guy, all six feet ten inches of him, has become an intermediary between my ex-wife and me in several areas of dispute.

Recently, I received a call asking me to meet him at his beachfront condo for a chat. I was suspicious, as neither of us had ever mastered the art of small talk. The conversation began on rather vague terms and suddenly swung to my ten-year-old little girl. I saw a tear fall from his eye as he disclosed that my former wife was soon going to be leaving for a job in the Hawaiian Islands. As a result, my daughter would soon be moving to the other side of the world!

I sank back into the chair and went totally numb. It all happened too fast. I was about to lose the only thing in the entire world that I cared about. My crying turned to sobbing, and we uttered no words for the longest time. That night as I drove back into the city, I felt my impending loss even greater and eventually fell asleep on a tear-stained pillow.

In the days since that night, I have set my mind to at least the appearance of being strong. My daughter will never know that inside I have died a thousand deaths. I could not even go to the airport to see her off that last day, for surely my mask would have split open for all to see. I have never before known the pain I felt during this time, and I have asked the Lord for comfort. As always, He has come to me.

> Who shall separate us from the love of
> Christ? Shall trouble or hardship or

persecution or famine or nakedness or danger or sword?

Romans 8: 35

MARCH 10, 1986

A few days after my 8th birthday, on a July afternoon, my dad took me to the old Episcopal Church down the street. We sat there together in a wooden pew, both of us awkwardly looking around but neither speaking. I stared up at the rafters, at timbers rough cut from ancient oaks with windows all around, intricately laced with gaudy colored glass and floors of burgundy velvet. The walls were wrapped in a rich tapestry of multi-colored banners draped from ceiling to floor while the smell of the place was never to be forgotten….an aroma of thick, stale incense, blended with air that had never known the sunlight. After a minute of deafening silence, he announced that I was soon to join the church and learn the catechism. Although I did not know what that was, I nodded affirmatively….I would have done anything to please him. It seems so odd now, looking backward at it all. He insisted that I join the church but cared little that I ever personally meet the man who spoke it into existence. That kind of moral calculus was not unusual for my father. It was always thus, that our family history is strewed with the bodies of those who lived only to present a public face….an outer garment that disintegrated into shame once the smoke had lifted. For he would not be the last man to cloak himself in the robes of religious belief….mistakenly choosing to build his life *near* the Kingdom of God, but not *around* it.

> Jesus said unto him, "Thou shalt love the Lord thy God
> with all thy heart, and with all thy soul, and with all thy mind.
> This is the first and great commandment."

Matthew 22: 37, 38

MARCH 14, 1986

We have all been hurt so much. Someone promised you their life and gave you only the afternoon. Someone promised you the world but would not allow you the ground you stand on. Someone promised you everything but could deliver on nothing. Parents swore their love, but withdrew, deciding you were not needing of it. Spouses vowed their love, but over time decided you were not worthy of it. Friends declared their love, until deciding you were not deserving of it. It was Christ the Lord who promised His love, knowing you were not even searching for it. No wonder we are perplexed over it all. No one else would even come our way. For when we speak of His devotion for us, we are momentarily lost for words to explain it. Perhaps it is because it is so wonderful, so incredible, so majestic, mere human sounds do not do it honor. For now we are in love with love itself and He who has come to us, when no one else would, is cherished beyond belief in the innermost sanctums of our hearts.

> In love he predestined us to be adopted as
> his sons through Jesus Christ, in accordance
> with his pleasure and will—to the praise of
> his glorious grace, which he has freely given
> us in the One he loves.

Ephesians 1: 4b, 5, 6

MARCH 19, 1986

I am a walking dead man. It is really a wonderful position in which to find yourself. Every day is lived as though it were the last. Dead men are much more alive than the "living."

By dying to self it is very possible to resist the overwhelming push to have others fulfill your every need. It is even more possible to give rather than receive. Life with God is so much richer than our perception of it, for where your treasure is, there also can be found your heart.

> I have been crucified with Christ and I no
> longer live, but Christ lives in me. The life I
> live in the body, I live by faith in the Son of
> God, who loved me and gave himself for me.
>
> Galatians 2: 20

MARCH 29, 1986

I was never able to understand it all. Everything was unraveling around me. There was not a day when I did not feel that all the forces of hell and a wealth of hypocrisy were firmly set in my path. The loosely formed union of in-laws and judicial courts had waged a five-year campaign against me where my victories were small or virtually non-existent. I was out-manned, out-maneuvered and placed in a defensive crouch at every crossing. The mindless judge who determined that small children are in better hands with their mothers in every divorced situation should be stoned.

Now, as a product of that absurd thinking, my daughter resides on the other side of the planet Earth. There is talk of "getting together" once or twice a year just to catch up on everything. Becoming more secluded every evening, I sit alone beside the fireplace recalling times goneby. Some nights find me lying on a field of grass, surveying the blanket of stars stretched out above me, wondering if He even remembers my name. After all, who am I that the Bright and Morning Star should care about so insignificant a creature as me? I am like a wave tossed about on the ocean, here today and gone tomorrow.

What a foolish man I am. Will I ever learn? Could the flowers forget to bloom or the leaves forget to fall? Could the wind forget to blow or the birds forget to sing? Could the hand forget to touch or the heart forget to love? Neither could the Lord our God forget those of us whom He brought back from the abyss of hell and recorded our names in the Book of Life.

> "Power always thinks it has a great soul and vast views beyond the comprehension of the weak; and that it is doing God's service, when it is violating ALL His Laws".

John Adams
February 2nd, 1816

APRIL 6, 1986

I was never quite able to entirely understand the bond forged over the years between my daughter and me. It was a gift from God, a mystery that evolved over time and never needed to be fully understood.

There were times when I would challenge myself to peel away the outer layer of our relationship and view what made it all tick. Some days I considered the union so special because she was an "only" child. Other times I reasoned that because I was now unmarried, there was more time to devote to the cause. Then one afternoon, quite unexpectedly, the veil lifted, and the inner workings of our special relationship became as transparent as glass.

In her face I could see my own. She was a small defenseless child, innocent and pure, lost and looking for someone older and bigger to show the way. Many years ago, when I needed that special person to come forward, there had been no one. Never again. I now have an opportunity to heal my own past by lifting my own daughter's hope for the future.

Arriving at such a realization was very liberating and sobering to my soul and from that day forward, we have never left each other's heart. While so many men my age sought greatness in the eyes of the world, I was very much content to find it in my own backyard.

> The path of the righteous is like the first
> gleam of dawn, shining ever brighter till the
> full light of day.
>
> Proverbs 4: 18

NOVEMBER 2, 1986

One may recall our earliest history, when primitive man escaped into the security of dark caves to protect himself from the awful world outside. Well, not much has changed over all these many years. I have spent much of my life in underground hollows in order to shield my emotions and my face from those around me. All of us are sometimes among the cave dwellers, are we not, like the moon whose dark side is seen by no one? As for myself, I have always known there was someone behind the curtain. I would often stare at that man in the mirror and ask him to talk to me. Although he rarely spoke, I felt him there. He is hidden by the veneer and the confusion of this life. His words, though few, are lost above the clatter of music and the clamor of cars speeding by. He is very much afraid and is lost in a world where he is a foreigner in his own land. So, he remains hidden in every shadow and, like Nicodemus, prefers the pitch black of night. He is hurt, but not destroyed…..sad, but not forlorn. His tears are commonplace, but all survivors have mastered the art of swimming to the shore. He wishes to tell you who he is. He hopes you will listen. He knows you will not.

> You are my hiding place; you will protect
> me from trouble and surround me with
> songs of deliverance.
>
> Psalm 32: 7

JUNE 5, 1987

My parents, even at their complete worst, were not totally blind to a life of faith. They attended sometimes but sent me often to the small church down the street near the water's edge. But as a small boy of eight, I was far more interested in what was going on outside the building than inside those hallowed halls. The sanctuary was constructed of beautiful red brick wrapped on the outside by greenery that grew so tall and thick that it hid the figures encased in stain-glassed windows.

Out by the roadside and surrounding the entire grounds, church officers had planted signs inviting the angels of the Lord to actually park their vehicles if they, and the rest of the heavenly host, were ever to visit there. It was years later, after I had learned to read better, that I realized my mistake. For the signs did *not* read "angel parking" but rather "angle parking".

> Do not forget to entertain strangers,
> for by so doing some people have
> entertained angels without knowing it.
>
> Hebrews 13: 2

JULY 9, 1987

My daughter, Sara, was born on Labor Day, 1976. We chose her name as a reflection of the Biblical wife of Abraham, whose name was actually spelled "Sarah." It was Abraham to whom the Lord made the promise, "In you, all the families of the earth shall be blessed," and indeed everyone who knows my daughter recognizes the seeds of greatness.

It is 1987, and our family has now been parted for six years. New lives and new loves have sprouted all around and among us. However, no amount of time or distance can change the fact that I wanted Sara back. I have consulted with some of the few friends who did not bolt in the days before and was advised to go easy. I have been told on more than one occasion to "wait upon the Lord" and encouraged to learn the art of "courageous waiting". I have made so many mistakes in the course of this life.... I will not add losing my only daughter to that list.

> To everything there is a season, and a time to every purpose under heaven: A time to be born, and a time to die......
> a time to weep and a time to laugh, a time to mourn and a time to dance, a time of war and a time of peace...

Ecclesiastes 3

AUGUST 2, 1987

My aspirations for Sara and me were never cloaked in secrecy. I made it very clear to anyone who asked that I thought it wiser to prepare your children for the path... rather than prepare the path for your children.

I met with my attorney and laid out a strategy wherein I would set forth the new agenda in a written document to be delivered to Sara's mother. There was no doubt that a collision of the minds was soon to take place. And indeed, one week after mailing the letter, I received the telephone call that would introduce me to new levels of anger while evoking memories of my turbulent past.

Nonetheless, her mother and I decided to meet at my home in the week following in order to settle the issue for good. I was understandably nervous during the days leading up to our meeting. I wanted to resume the daily roll of father. But, more than anything, I wanted to oversee the teenage years of my daughter's life that were set directly before us. Many years earlier I had been robbed of my own childhood; now, I refused to have my daughter's childhood also stolen away from me. I was determined, no matter the price, to set us both free.

> Blessed are those who hunger and thirst for
> righteousness, for they will be filled. Blessed
> are the merciful, for they will be shown mercy.
> Blessed are the pure in heart, for they will see God.
> Blessed are the peacemakers, for they will be
> called sons of God. Blessed are those who are
> persecuted because of righteousness, for theirs
> is the Kingdom of Heaven.
>
> Matthew 5: 6, 7, 8, 9, 10

AUGUST 10, 1987

The meeting, if you can call it that, was strained and awkward. Sara's mother brought her 68 year-old father along for moral support. We sat in my living room glaring back and forth at each other while exchanging small talk. Finally, we got to the business at hand. Clearly, the years had changed both her mother and me. She had not remarried and was no longer the confident, aspiring single who demanded that everyone provide her "her space." I had grown stronger and more assured with each passing day and felt my cause was more than noble and worthy of the momentary clumsiness of the situation.

Two hours had passed when we shook hands and parted company. The battle had been won! It was, without question, the greatest victory of my life. I walked outside. The sky had never seemed so blue before, and the soft summer breeze was all for me.

On that glorious day there were neither marching bands nor streamers in the air. But the sweet scent of vindication was mine. It poured across my lighted face and mixed with the cool elixir of recovered purpose. For once, for once, the good guys won!

> Trust in the Lord with all your heart and lean
> not on your own understanding; in all your
> ways acknowledge him, and he will make
> your paths straight.
>
> Proverbs 3: 5, 6

AUGUST 20, 1987

Having lived my days as a boy among raging alcoholics, my own view of parenting has been shaped and honed. The "experts" told me that I would most likely become a slave and turn out just like my mother and father. On hearing that, I decided these "experts" would have to be wrong. Everything I did, every single decision I made, would be 180 degrees in the opposite direction.

I set my mind that I would never be the type of parent my mother and father came to be. I have lived every day in the shadow of that promise to myself, resolving never to make such foolish mistakes with the lives of other people. However, my parents unwittingly taught me a valuable lesson. Careers will come and go, possessions rust and burn, but your children are the delight of life itself. While many have turned their backs on me and walked away, my own child turned toward me and held out her hand. Because of that supreme act of trust, I will spend every cent I have and every moment remaining, telling her how very, very honored that has made me.

Kids want money; they want friends; but more than all other things, they want absolute, unconditional love. Their guts cry out for it. Show it to your kids, and they will follow you to the end of the earth. Many parents are caught up in a cycle of scolding and finger pointing. I wanted to get away from all of that.

As a boy, the thing I desired above all others was to be accepted. I wanted acceptance when I was good or bad, right or wrong, dirty or clean. Knowing full well that I would have crossed the oceans to find it, I decided from the beginning to give this gift, unconditional acceptance, to my wonderful daughter as the centerpiece of our relationship. Nothing, absolutely nothing, could replace my love for her. And while I did not possess great material wealth, I could give my love as a legacy of my own terrible childhood where it was denied to me. While it is true that I have made many mistakes, this decision became the crown jewel in the helmet known as fatherhood.

Blessed are you when people insult you, persecute
you and falsely say all kinds of evil against you
because of me. Rejoice and be glad, because great
is your reward in heaven, for in the same way
they persecuted the prophets who were before you.

Matthew 5: 11, 12

SEPTEMBER 22, 1987

As I write these words, the family is together again...the father, the daughter, and the overweight cocker spaniel named Pogo. I have always loved dogs. This pup has often been my only companion over the years, and his faithfulness should be a lesson to us all. I guess I feel a certain kind of kinship with him.

Throughout much of my own life, I have been made to feel much like a stray dog. There were so many times when I had nothing to eat, no place to sleep, and no one to care for me. I have been rejected by my owners, adopted, and then sent out again into the freezing cold. I roamed the back streets and alleys, thinking that one day I might finally find a real home.

Then one day, something wonderful happened! I met a man who said I was no longer to be cast aside. He called me a purebred. He cleaned me up, fed me, and treated me as if He really loved me. No wonder they call him The Savior.

> And everyone who has left houses or
> brothers or sisters or father or mother or
> children or fields for my sake will receive
> a hundred times as much and will inherit
> eternal life. But many who are first will be
> last, and many who are last will be first.
>
> Matthew 19: 29, 30

OCTOBER 2, 1988

I am continually puzzled by this singular question: Why me? Why did the Father not pick the passenger to my left on the bus? I am not worthy. I am selfish, arrogant, foolish, and lazy. My faults stretch as far as the East is from the West. What he sees in me, I do not know.

However, I am aware of this most important fact: Christ loves me and cares for me in a way no one ever has or ever could. It overwhelms me each day to walk the face of this earth and watch as the doors open before my very eyes.

His love for me calls for a word bigger than love alone could ever express. He is truly the father I never had. When earthly death comes for me, dear friends, do not weep. For I desire to look into His eyes much closer than I ever have before.

Lord, if only I could express how much my love is yours. You are beyond the beyond yet close enough to touch. You prepared the universe, as it knew we were coming. In the rains your arms are outstretched above my head....in my sorrows you wrap me in the fold of your garment. You are my protector and you are my shield. And while time may wrinkle my skin and blind my eyes, I will never forget the kindness I have known. As surely as the wave seeks the shore, I will come to you. I have never before known a friend like you, someone whose arms were always opened and whose door was never closed. Before you, I knew nothing but the assurance of my own oblivion....since you, I have known only your peace. Father, create in me that which I do not possess and stir up in me that which desires to slumber. For I wish to be so weak that my flesh no longer seeks to steal the glory of the Lord.

How will I ever thank you for your truth, which moved when I moved and lured me from the cocoon of my own selfishness? How will I ever repay for the gift that brought me to your doorstep and unleashed the never ending joy of knowing that my heart was captured by yours? What human words can I speak that will tell you of my adoration? I cannot run fast enough to find you when the day awakes, and in the night

I have no other lover but you. The songwriter said it better than I ever could.... *"there were bells on the hill, but I never heard them ringing, no I never heard them at all, til there was you"*.....

He is known to many as the Beginning and the End. Indeed, He is the Alpha and Omega. He is the gentleness of every breeze, the blue of every sky, the melody of every song. He is the sweetness of every smile, the warmth of every fire, the hunger of every heart. He is everything to me.

> For God so loved the world that he gave his
> one and only Son, that whoever believes in
> him shall not perish but have eternal life.

John 3: 16

MAY 6, 1989

My new life as father is better than I could have ever hoped it would be. I drink from the saucer as my cup overflows with the goodness of God. Days roll into weeks, and all is wonderfully mundane. I am like a soldier whose years of duty at the front have brought him to yearn for the solitude of peace. And yet, the conflict still rages, not about me, but around me.

I spoke recently with a neighbor who had left his wife and three small children. His face showed no remorse or concern and his words were dripping with contempt. He noted that there was a very good reason for his sudden departure...a beautiful young girl and the thrill of singleness. He rambled on about losing, *not* his family, but a house, belongings, and the car. But oddly, all was well because he had traded it all for what he now had gained...happiness. His words caused me to reflect on my own past. There were those anguished days when a younger man toyed with the delectable notion of disappearing into the night, but could never actually do it.

So I ask, how does a person acquire happiness by turning his back on his own people? Can happiness be gained by staring into the eyes of your own beautiful children and announcing to them that they have lost their father to a sweeter, gentler face?

As for myself, may I always choose to stay the course, to resist the pull of self. Today I bathe freely in the soft warm light of right thinking. I can look confidently into the eyes of all whom I meet and know that promises kept are the backbone of all good men.

> Blessed are the people of whom this is true;
> Blessed are the people whose God is the Lord.

Psalm 144: 15

NOVEMBER 16, 1990

Many months have passed since I last placed words into this journal. While I have had many things to say, I chose of my own volition to remain silent. And life of recent has been so free and undemanding that it is immensely difficult to do anything but enjoy its unstoppable rhythm. The once angry young man has grown older and mellows even more with every passing hour.

However, there is not a day that passes when I do not ask the Lord to sit with me in the cool of the evening, long after the shadows have slithered away and the dusk is waiting for the night. There by the light of the stars, which He placed in the heavens, I speak my mind to Him. "Would you give me another chance? Would you let me go back and start all over again?" My shoulders slump forward. It must be very difficult, I think, to give another car to a hit and run driver. I have made a legion of mistakes throughout my lifetime. Have I been carried this far only to die in silence?

> I will repay you for the years the locusts
> have eaten...You will have plenty to eat,
> until you are full, and you will praise the
> name of the Lord your God, who has worked
> wonders for you; never again will my people
> be shamed.
>
> Joel 2: 25a, 26

FEBRUARY 13, 1991

In the early days, before my own journey down that winding road to Damascus, I was neither a lover nor hater of my world. I really just did not care. For to me, life was lived day to day, surviving one ordeal then pausing only to gather strength to encounter the next. Since the earliest of days, my path had been strewn with thorns and my very life threatened by those who had sworn to remain at my side. One does not fret about the weeks ahead if one dreads the approaching night. I often heard of the fisherman and His nail-scarred hands…that he was the good in all our lives. But within the walls of our home we were consumed by endless confusions about the past and had no vision for any future. From those whom you would expect to find it, I saw no goodness, nor kindness, nor mercy. So, it should be of no surprise that I learned to doubt that such a figure as the "life giver" even existed. And, if He did, I could not believe that He would even want me….scarred, broken, and thrown out with the trash, as I was. Overtime, I began to consider that the persecution that I came to know was perhaps the Lord's gift to me. Then one day, Jesus stood before, in all His majesty saying, "Thomas, put your finger here and see the wounds of love in my hands". And on that glorious day, I strapped on the breastplate of righteousness, in remembrance of the shed blood of the Son of the Most High God. I stepped then into the shoes of peace, that I might stand strong in the good news of the coming of the Christ. I lifted before me the shield of faith, that I might be prepared for the lies and deceit of this fallen world. Finally, I donned the helmet of salvation, that I would remain true and faithful to He who had called me out of darkness into His wonderful light.

Thomas said to Him, "My Lord and my God"
Then Jesus told him
"Because you have seen me
you have believed; blessed
are those who have not seen
and yet have believed."

John 20: 28, 29

AUGUST 6, 1993

While difficult to say, I found much sin both "inside" and "outside" the community of the faithful. Sometimes I even confronted people about things that were going on, and they used the occasion to make a subtle confession. Then there were others whose serial confessions just brought on serial sinning, and I concluded that there are babes in Christ whose excesses will always be part of the fabric of a broken people. I came to understand that some believers had, in their minds, arranged a kind of penance system, wherein it was appropriate to commit acts of any extreme as long as that was "offset" by a similar act of generosity or servant hood. After having tasted the sweetness of the Lord, the various sins that had marred my past would daily haunt me, murmuring soft and alluring words of "I am here".....and I would summon the courage to answer, "But, you see, It is no longer I". For he whom the Lord sets free....is free indeed.

Then there was the case of my friend Philip Johnson. I met Philip at a local church where we both were involved with the singles ministry. He always spoke of his dissatisfaction with life and his unmet need to find a wife and eventually have a family. Philip and I read and shared the gospel together every Tuesday evening for over four months until he, without notice, simply decided to stop meeting with me. A month later, Johnson robbed his own employer, an armored car carrier, and disappeared across the southern border into Mexico. His theft of 22 million dollars remains, even today, the biggest heist in the history of the United States. Five months after the incident, Philip was caught reentering the United States at the Texas border and is today serving a 35 year sentence for kidnapping and armed robbery. I attempted on multiple occasions to find out where he was incarcerated so that I could write him but was never given his location. I am reminded again that the road to Damascus is littered with the bodies of those who chose not to complete the journey.

All of us will be presented a life choice. Pray God that our decision will be right.

> Two roads diverged in a wood, and I…
> I took the one less traveled by,
> and that has made all the difference.
>
> Robert Frost
> "The road not taken"

MARCH 30, 1994

As a divorced, single adult, I have looked extensively for a place to meet people who shared my point of view. The first group that I encountered invited me to a dinner where the "entire divorced population of our city will be present." That sounded great. Arriving ten minutes early to insure my place at the table, I was startled to find only eleven people present in the dining hall. To make matters worse, I was the only one in the group who still possessed his original set of teeth.

Fortunately, persistence did pay off. I soon found the "Seekers," a fun group of men and women with whom I had much in common. Many of my concepts of life after divorce were formulated while being surrounded by those great people. While in Seekers, I had the unique opportunity to actually minister to the newcomers, those who had recently found themselves no longer among the married.

Within the community of these believers were two distinct groups. First, were the "lookers," the strong who could put words together well and seemed never to be afraid. Then, there were the "others." These folks usually arrived unkempt, unshaven, and seemed quite satisfied to find themselves relegated to the role of followers. The paradox unfolded before my eyes very slowly. It was only years later that I even really saw it. It was the story of the tortoise and the hare. For the "lookers" were distracted by everything and everyone that came their way, and those whom I had pegged as mere "followers" were just that…"followers" of the Prince of Peace.

> Do not be yoked together with unbelievers.
> For what do righteousness and wickedness
> have in common? Or what fellowship can
> light have with darkness?

II Corinthians 6: 14

APRIL 6, 1994

For such a long time I was convinced that I was the heir to an empty kingdom. My parents had allowed virtually all of their worldly possessions to be dissolved in the pursuit of momentary pleasures. There was little left for those of us who came behind.

Then I awoke one morning to find I was the son of the King. Not just any king, you understand. This King is the ruler of all that is and all that ever shall be. He is like no other, a father to us all. He holds the hand of all who sigh and wipes the tears of those who cry. For our pleasure He placed a million dancing fireflies in the moonlit sky and all the cattle on every hill are His. And for those of us, who are subjects in His vast and mighty dominion, *every* day is Father's Day.

> The Spirit himself testifies with our spirit
> that we are God's children. Now if we are
> children, then we are heirs—heirs of God
> and co-heirs with Christ, if indeed we share
> in his sufferings in order that we may also
> share in his glory.
>
> Romans 8: 16, 17

MAY 28, 1994

Sara graduated from high school yesterday. Her father was proud beyond words. In the early days, she was shifted from school to school, from state to state, playing the game of divorce merry-go-round. Yesterday, she stepped to the podium as Senior Class Valedictorian, raising the bar for all who will follow. Webster long ago ran out of adjectives to describe how wonderful she is and I am unable to adequately express how much I love her. I drafted some thoughts on paper, thinking she might include them in her prepared remarks to her fellow classmates. However, when I heard her final delivery, I was glad she had passed me over. I liked her words far, far more than my own.

> He giveth power to the faint; and to them
> that have no might, he increases their strength.
> But they that wait upon the lord shall renew
> their strength…they shall mount up with wings
> as eagles, they shall run and not be weary.
>
> Isaiah 40: 29, 31

FEBRUARY 17, 1995

When I first set off on this journey known as fatherhood, I found sure footing on this time-tested principle: Fathers produce children. Simply stated, in me, my daughter would see the world beyond the backyard fence, and I would set her upon my knee and try to explain all things that were unexplainable. Parents instinctively know that they cannot properly raise a child if they are unwilling to be occasionally scorned. But as our lives over time became wrapped together, a discernible shift in my thinking emerged. Stepping back and seeing the big picture, it was obvious to all that I had become the student and she the teacher. I could not help but notice the eloquence with which she conducted every aspect of her life. I quietly marveled at it all.

So, I gladly confess the error of my thinking. For I have learned from her far more than I ever could have revealed. Much wiser now, I joyfully announce that fathers do not produce children, but rather that children produce fathers. Amen.

> She speaks with wisdom, and faithful instruction is on her tongue. She watches over the affairs of her household and does not eat the bread of idleness. Her children arise and call her blessed; her husband also, and he praises her; Many women do noble things, but you surpass them all.
>
> Proverbs 31: 26, 27, 28, 29

Tommy as a freshman in college

Tommy and Sara, 1981

the author guiding a backhand across the net

Sara as a high school senior

Sara before the Prom, 1994

dad and daughter at home together

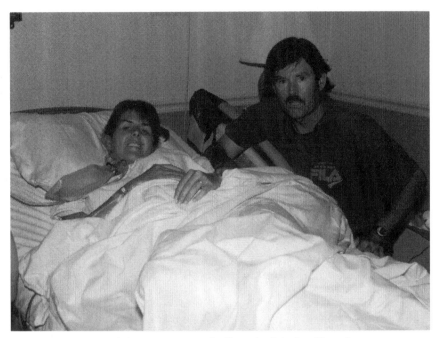

Tommy and Sara moments before the birth of her first son

Sara, Clay, Scott, Emmi and Riley Black

Tommy and five-time Wimbledon Champion, Bjorn Borg

MARCH 2, 1996

My critics come from every point on the compass and they are as predictable as the tide. Many of their complaints are quite valid. I entered this life with the pure intent of taking from it as much as I could get away with and giving back as little as would be required of me. There were times in the selfishness of my younger days when I could see neither the forest *nor* the trees.

The Lord did change me, but those who knew me before, well, they will take their opinion of me to their graves. I cannot change anyone but myself and that remains a work in progress. But I have won the race, crossing every stream and landing feet first in the land promised to us from the very beginning of time. I refuse to lose when I can win. I refuse to embrace a lie when such a high price was paid that I might intimately know the Truth. My only regret is that I stood alone at the dock when, at last, my ship came in. Here among the broken and the bruised, I have found that peace which hides its face from so many. Contentment greets me at every dawn and joy kisses me goodnight at every sunset.

> Take nothing for the journey except a staff-
> no bread, no bag, no money in your belts.
> Wear sandals but not an extra tunic.
> Whenever you enter a house, stay there until
> you leave that town. And if any place will
> not welcome you or listen to you, shake the
> dust off your feet when you leave, as a
> testimony against them.

Mark 6: 8, 9, 10, 11

AUGUST 3, 1996

I have a very close friend who is an archenemy. His name is Unforgiveness. For years we have worked together, played together, and worshipped together. We have been a couple through thick and thin and sadly, often cuddled in the hush of night. Furthermore, as you might expect, we have had our good days and bad.

In recent times, I have seen my companion differently. Now he is old and very ugly, with sharp features, grotesque and frightening. Indeed, his friendship over time has slowed me down, labored every move, and taxed my every emotion.

It is time for this so-called "friend" and I to go our separate ways. Please, Father, show me the way.

> For if you forgive men when they sin against
> you, your heavenly Father will also forgive
> you.
>
> Matthew 6: 14

NOVEMBER 18, 1996

He is a mystery to some, this Jesus of Nazareth. So I ask, "How is it that we can truly love someone whom we have not actually embraced in the flesh?" The answer, of course, is right before our eyes. In Him, we know great heights for we have walked with Him through the valley of despair. In Him, we know great joy, for we have acquainted ourselves with so many of His sorrows. In Him, we now know wonderful liberty, for we have chained our hearts to the freedom of His love.

So, while we have not yet embraced Him in the flesh, we daily seek to embrace Him in the spirit. In so doing, we have fallen in love, not with that which the eye sees, but rather with that which the heart knows. It is in this assurance that the embers of love smolder every day and every moment inside our beings.

> For I am convinced that neither death nor
> life, neither angels nor demons, neither the
> present nor the future, nor any powers,
> neither height nor depth, nor anything else in
> all creation, will be able to separate us from
> the love of God that is in Christ Jesus our
> Lord.
>
> Romans 8: 38, 39

DECEMBER 21, 1996

Today was a day unlike all others. On this glorious day, I walked the aisle as father of the bride. If pride was a ball of light, all of those who were present should have been blinded this day. My thoughts drifted back to the early days when my own young life seemed to hang each moment in limbo. How very happy I now found myself, as I realized one of my own has succeeded where I have stumbled and fallen. The circle of evil is broken here, never again to strike those who have run so far to escape it.

The journey to this place has taken me over every bump on every road. It was a trip I began as a boy and finally completed as a man. This gathering of family and friends has brought me tears of hope and sadness fused with other emotions too deep and too tangled to confront. "Now the job is done," I thought; "Now the old soldier can lay down his sword." Perhaps it is time for peace to spread throughout the land.

There will never be enough training for fatherhood; one lifetime is simply not enough. As fathers, we have tried our very best and ask only to be judged with boundless mercy. But we cannot escape the truth, the realization that all the daily tribulations have now become lost in time and only mountaintops remain. Over the years, I am sure every father has looked closely into the deep recesses of his own being and finally yielded to a new way of doing things. That is, laying down your own life every morning for those who have always been there and refusing to pick it up again. In so doing, the very word *father* will no longer be a title, but rather a glorious sound that forever elicits wonderful memories from those who have always known the truth.

> I have fought the good fight, I have finished the race, I have kept the faith. Now there is in store for me the crown of righteousness, which the Lord, the righteous Judge, will award to me on that day—and not only to

me, but also to all who have longed for
His appearing.

II Timothy 4: 7, 8

DECEMBER 23, 1996

There can be no doubt that my greatest weakness was the ever present need to seek the validation of men rather than the Prince. For it was always true that I would never seriously consider the sweetness of the Lord until I was strapped down in His presence with no where else to go. And since spending quiet time with Him was so difficult for me, I often wondered if He did not allow me to get into trouble just so He could hear from me once in a while.

So, what is the cost of laying down your life every morning? Well, there will be some friendships you will never know, some lovemaking you will never do, some sights you will never see. But there will also be some trouble you will never find, some evil you will never meet, some hole into which you will never fall, some tears you will never cry. And I must always remind myself that there is really only an audience of One. And He has shown me time and time again that His stars can still be seen quite clearly.....even from the deepest well.

> Humble yourselves, therefore, under
> God's mighty hand that he may lift you
> up in due time. Cast all your care upon
> Him, for he cares for you.
>
> 1 Peter 5: 6, 7

DECEMBER 24, 1996

I have often wondered in the years since my own parent's passing, if they had any vision at all how their life choices would come to haunt me in adulthood. Did they, for instance, realize they had left me an emotional cripple at times, struggling with marital intimacy, self-worth, and a purpose for being? Did they realize that unsettled issues of youth would bring me, more than once, to question my own desire to live? But in having to consider it so often, I did sharpen my own awareness of the role parents play in the lives of their children and grandchildren.

I observed that those obscure, seemingly unimportant decisions we make everyday do in fact play out fully in the generations that will follow. And we demonstrate our complete dedication to their success by walking in daily sacrifice...putting aside our own momentary passions to assure that those who follow will have a firm path and clear channel to show the way. It is unfortunate that some mothers and fathers, shortsighted in their own view of life, have provided a legacy of misfortune and chaos for those they purport to "live for." These families are like dominoes, one generation spiraling out of control, its sinfulness crashing into the next, claiming victim after victim. It is for those of us who will refuse to be swept away in this flood of generational squalor, who choose to climb the highest mountain, warning others of the danger below. We need to insist, if need be, that the dying stop now...that we live from this moment forward in peace with our Father, the maker of Heaven and Earth. We shall proclaim to all who will listen that the past can no longer dictate what is to come; that we will no longer see with eyes of discord and hate, for our destiny requires us to embrace all who commonly share the breath of life. And when the final chapter is written, let it be said of us that we did not come this far to have walked the walk in vain.

> And anyone who does not take his cross and
> follow me is not worthy of me. Whoever

finds his life will lose it, and whoever loses his life for my sake will find it.

Matthew 10: 38, 39

DECEMBER 25, 1996

It is Christmas day. The whole world over celebrates the birth of the Christ child 2,000 years ago in Bethlehem. For those of us who call these United States "home," the joy of this date has an additional distinctive meaning...

Come back with me to December 25, 1776. George Washington's gutsy band of fighters, the Continentals and local militia, have been soundly routed at every confrontation with the British. Tired and weary, they, along with the Commander-in-Chief, stumble back across the frozen Delaware River to recuperate from the beatings at the hands of the Redcoats. Their marches have left a trail of red in the glistening snow, as few have shoes and blood seeps through the burlap bags wrapped around their swollen feet. Washington is lost and confused as to how to turn. His hand trembles as he scratches out a message by candlelight to be sent by courier back to Congress, finishing it with, "I think the game is pretty nearly up" (Irving, 324). The smell of death and talk of mutiny is in the air. Can anything, he wonders, be done to rescue this fledgling attempt at self-rule from perishing here in the freezing snow? Washington secretly convenes his top officers to try one last time, one final gasp of hope, crossing back across the Delaware on Christmas night and surprising the enemy garrisons at Trenton. Before departing, he reminds those around him in hushed tones of the American password this night..."Victory or death!"

The history books tell the rest of the story. That night, December 25, 1776, a small American force led by George Washington, crossed the ice-choked Delaware River and captured the British outpost at Trenton, New Jersey. And from that moment forward, the American cause was not to be stopped, culminating with the surrender of the British army under Cornwallis five years later at Yorktown, Virginia.

It is a wonderful day! We celebrate with joy unspeakable. For on this day was born the Prince of Peace to show us the way home. And on this date in 1776, was born this country we love, our "home away from home", that shining city on a hill, the land of our fathers..... the home of the brave.

Patrick Henry, March 23, 1775......

"Sir, we are not weak if we make a proper use of those means which the God of nature hath placed in our power. The millions of people, armed in the holy cause of liberty, and in such a country as that which we possess, are invincible by any force which our enemy can send against us. Besides, Sir......we shall not fight our battles alone. There is a just God, who presides over the destinies of nations, and who will raise up friends to fight our battles for us. The battle, sir, is not to the strong alone; it is to the vigilant, the active and the brave!"

And she brought forth her firstborn son, and wrapped him in swaddling clothes, and laid him in a manger; because there was no room for them in the inn. And there were in the same country shepherds abiding in the field, keeping watch over their flock by night. And lo, the angel of the Lord came upon them, and the Glory of the Lord shone round about them: and they were sore afraid. And the angel said unto them, fear not: for, behold I bring you good tidings of great joy, which shall be to all people. For unto you is born this day in the city of David a Savior, which is Christ the Lord.

Luke 2: 7, 8, 9, 10, 11

DECEMBER 26, 1996

I do not know why I had never taken notice of it before, but it is so very clear to me now. The purposes of the Lord are bigger, deeper, wider and never fully revealed or understood by simple men. On the afternoon of October 9, 1781, General George Washington put a match to the first blast of canon aimed at the British war machine hunkered down in Yorktown. And for the next week, day and night, there came from the Americans and their French allies, a never-ending cannonade. So severe was the onslaught that Lord Cornwallis quickly found his quarters and his fortunes tumbling in around him. Mercifully, on the 17th of October, a small boy climbed to the top of the British position carrying a white flag, and, for all practical purposes, the American war for independence came to an end. The number of prisoners taken were 7,073, of whom 5,950 were enlisted men while the others were English officers. The surrender ceremony took place two days later. The French and American Armies were drawn up in a line more than a mile long, with the French on one side of the road and the Americans on the other. At one o'clock in the afternoon, the defeated British garrisons marched out of Yorktown proper and passed into a large field, their column forced to proceed between the victors on the right and left. The British officers, at one select point yelled "ground arms", and the rank and file soldiers threw down their muskets, some breaking them on the ground while their drummers beat out the tune of *"The World turned Upside Down"*. Many of the vanquished openly wept at the humiliation of so great a loss at the hands of such a rabble as they perceived the Americans to be. It is difficult for us in the here and now to fully appreciate the range of emotions there so many years ago at Yorktown. However, imagine the army of the greatest military force on earth bending the knee to a country that, in 1781, existed only on paper in the form of the Declaration of Independence. For, in truth, the Americans had no designated capitol, no viable currency, no king, and no government to speak of. And worse, most of the American regiment that lined the road that warm October day stood in tattered rags, and only a few possessed a simple pair of shoes. That these elite British warriors would feel the ultimate humiliation should be of no surprise to anyone.

It is only in the enlightening hindsight of history that we can see the hand of God. For the country that won the day, The United States of America, would grow to become the greatest military power that ever existed on the face of the earth. And the descendants of the victorious at Yorktown would, 163 years later, cross the Atlantic to rescue all of Europe from the satanic grip of Nazi Germany.

It is a truth that could *never* have been conceived by the "humiliated" at Yorktown.

For, had there been no America, there may have no longer existed a British empire in the latter half of the twentieth century.

> Oh give thanks to the Lord, for He is good.
> For His loving kindness is everlasting.
> Let the redeemed of the Lord say so.
> Whom He has redeemed from the hand of the adversary,
> and gathered from the lands, from the east and from the west,
> from the north and from the south.

Psalm 107: 1, 2, 3

DECEMBER 30, 1996

It is worth being mindful that this overwhelming need for "completeness" in all of us begins in the external realm. I guess we assume it will arrive one day, miraculously, on the inner part of our being. We seek wealth to attain security, beauty to acquire confidence, a companion to feel needed, and religion to claim a form of emotional peace. And then one day, when these impostors have all died and fallen away, we stumble, bleeding and injured, into the Truth.

Wealth can be lost in a day, beauty eventually deserts everyone, companions will surely disappoint us, and religion is a counterfeit from the bowels of hell.

There is only One who brings fullness of heart, completeness of spirit and freely disperses peace that surpasses all human understanding. He is *always* present, *always* faithful, *always* in love, *always* the same........ He is Jesus Christ the Lord. Amen.

> Remember your leaders, who spoke the word
> of God to you. Consider the outcome of their
> way of life and imitate their faith.
> Jesus Christ is the same yesterday and today
> and forever. Do not be carried away by all
> kinds of strange teachings.

Hebrews 13: 8

MARCH 1, 1997

I hope to live one day in a place where the rejected are instead the received, where the word "hate" is never spoken, where only the demons are demonized. I hope to live one day in a place where greatness is commonplace and "honor" is the rule rather than the exception. A place where great love is synonymous with great sacrifice and "selfishness" a plague to be avoided at all cost. I hope to live one day in a place where the unborn need never fear the executioner's knife, and children come to know "home" as the fulfillment of every dream. A place where one's own happiness is not bought at the price of another's pain…a place where the value of a man is measured by the depth of his character, not by the color of his skin. I hope to live one day where those who know God as friend are not portrayed as fools, and humbleness is the mark of every man. A place where the power of love reigns over the love of power and where eyes cry only tears of joy. I have not yet approached the outskirts of such a place; surely, it must be Heaven.

> Behold, I will create new heavens and a
> new earth. The former things will not be
> remembered, nor will they come to mind.
> But be glad and rejoice forever in what I
> will create, for I will create Jerusalem to
> be a delight and its people a joy.

Isaiah 65: 17, 18

JANUARY 6, 1998

So where does the strength come from to see each conflict through? It is deep within every one of us, exposed in the heat of battle where each layer of vulnerability is meticulously peeled away.

As for me, I am hopefully drawing closer to becoming that man of velvet and steel, wisdom and virtue, those endearing qualities we pray for in every son. Now at age fifty-four, retirement is surely just around the corner; and I wait eagerly for the blissful days of an endless summer.

Be joyous and live each day to its fullest. However, heed this word of caution: Beware of those who, without remorse, crucify both their conscience and their honor on the altar of "self." They will have their reward. Trust in God the Almighty. From His hands will come the final touch of glory to deliver us all. Our future is *not* written in the stars....... instead, it lies in the hands of the Lord who made them.

> Let us fix our eyes on Jesus, the author and perfecter of our faith, who for the joy set before him endured the cross, scorning its shame, and sat down at the right hand of the Throne of God.
>
> Hebrews 12: 2

JUNE 11, 1999

It has been some time since I have lifted this pen. Sara and her husband, Scott, are beginning their lives together in their new house near Chattanooga, Tennessee. I, myself, am in the final months of a career that began forty years ago on a dusty tennis court one hot, sultry, summer afternoon. But, enough about us. What about those of you who will read these words? I am confident that each of you has mentally recorded a similar diary, perhaps not yet put on paper. At any rate, there can be no doubt that each of us will have a chance to choose the way we live, and our choices will write the story of our lives. Some of you will elect to go out on your own, heeding the advice of no one, grabbing life by the throat and demanding that it submit to your every need. Others will become bystanders, having a casual opinion and secretly wishing that all their hopes would someday come to pass. And still others will be knocked to the ground again and again, rising courageously each time, never allowing "right" to be called "wrong" or evil to be viewed with eyes of goodness. Bury me here among the living saints. They are the bravest in the land, those boys and girls, men and women, who see each day as a hillside to be taken, a mountain to be mastered.

To those of you who dedicate your life to the mocking of the only God who can rip the blindfold from your eyes, I say, "Beware." For you, dear friend, are like a well without water or a cloud without rain. And you shall be forced to confront your foolishness, not only in this present life, but all the way to the end of the age that has not yet even begun! As for the rest of us, sleep well. For as surely as one eye is on the sparrow, the other watches over you.

> As the deer pants for streams of water, so
> my soul pants for you, O God.
>
> Psalm 42: 1

SEPTEMBER 5, 1999

It is in the providence of God that I will soon be joining my daughter, Sara, in our joint effort to build a tennis program in southern Tennessee. I cannot wait to begin. It is like being "born again" again. I now see a chance to wipe the slate clean, to clear the ledger of old accounts and begin everything anew. Desperately needed are new challenges, fresh fields to conquer..... . for my past is much like an albatross around my neck. I do not want to simply survive, nor will it be enough to only endure. For when the last chapter has been scribbled down, I can rest in peace knowing that I did, in fact, prevail. For our story is not about how we died, rather it is all about how we lived.

> Taste and see that the Lord is good; blessed
> is the man who takes refuge in him.

Psalm 34: 8

DECEMBER 19, 1999

To my beloved daughter Sara:
Sara, I would ask that you tuck this letter away somewhere and keep it for you and your children to read another day. You and I know this happens, for we both have seen letters written by my grandfather to my father that opened our eyes as to what was happening in their lives on that particular day.

Sara, today I am walking away from my position here in Florida after twenty years of service. I well remember my first few months and years here...your mother was in the process of ending our relationship and there were times when I was not sure I could make it to the next day. The joy in my life came from knowing that soon I would see you—that little, bouncing girl, who would pop out of your aunt's car and into the pro shop on Friday afternoons. Little could you know it at the time, but that was really my only reason to see the next day. I remember also, in 1996, leaving you there in Tennessee, with you waving goodbye from the porch of the old log cabin. I cried all the way home. Now, here as I leave both my career and this state behind, I cannot tell you in words how happy I am that our paths have crossed once more. I have absolutely no doubt that this will be the highlight of my working life. Additionally, I delight everyday that my new name will be "Gramps." So, as I say goodbye today to old friends, I relish in the thought of being close again to you, Scott, and the grandkids yet unnamed. I will always love you............

Daddy

> I waited patiently for the Lord; he turned to
> me and heard my cry. He lifted me out of
> the slimy pit, out of the mud and mire; he set
> my feet on a rock and gave me a firm place
> to stand. He put a new song in my mouth, a
> hymn of praise to our God. Many will see
> and fear and put their trust in the Lord.

Psalm 40: 1, 2, 3

FEBRUARY 3, 2000

The day finally arrived when I would need to say goodbye to the city that I had called "home" for the better part of fifty years. I loaded the last few things, including the dog, and drove out toward the major highway with my car heading north. Within minutes, I neared the city limits. Pulling to the roadside, I stared motionless into the rear view mirror. For the many wonderful people whom I would probably never see again, I spoke a prayer of thanks, and for those who had seen no need for my existence, I forgave them. Then stepping out of the car, I shook off the dust from my feet, and without another backward glance, pointed the car toward the glorious mountains of Tennessee and drove on for hours in absolute silence.

In the many years of living alone, I had learned that loneliness is not the absence of affection, but rather the absence of direction. I often thought of myself as George Bailey of *It's A Wonderful Life.* You see, when I had believed that everything was completely lost, only then did it really just begin. While I had believed that I was very much alone, in truth, I was never out of sight of the angels sent to watch over me. While I had believed that I was very much unwanted, in truth, I was adored by the Creator of all that ever was. And while I had believed that my future was no more, in truth, my very name had been written in the Book of Life. Now, I have more than known the Glory of God. No longer can I rise early to witness the dawn without bathing in His unending mercy. No more can I smell the rose without the remembrance of His majestic sweetness. Never again can I embrace His peace without reflecting over His overwhelming sacrifice. He is mine, I am His, and where I end He begins. One song writer wrote that He is *"More than Wonderful."* However, I say He is much, much more than that. For, over time, I have come to realize that God's incredible gift to us had been to sweep up our entire family into His arms and gently lead us into the knowledge of His Son. What greater act of love could He have chosen...keeping us safe here on Earth and sealing us together for all eternity in the Kingdom of the Most High God.

Behold, I am coming soon! My reward is with me, and I will give to everyone according to what he has done. I am the Alpha and the Omega, the First and the Last, the Beginning and the End.

Revelation 22: 12, 13

FEBRUARY 5, 2000

My arrival in southern Tennessee was fairly uneventful. Suffering from a case of bronchitis, I labored each day this week at the simplest task. Tonight, after nightfall, I stepped out into the yard and viewed, for the first time, the brilliant lights of Lookout Mountain illuminated high off in the distance. It is no wonder to me that the people of Tennessee speak so glowingly of their land—it is a paradise. Sometimes late in the evening, I take my weary mind and my dog for a ride through the narrow winding back roads of Hamilton County, along vine-draped Old Lee Highway to Apison Pike, crossing back to Ringgold Road and returning through the pass along Standifer Gap. It is a private moment, a time to unload the concerns and run away from the weight of the past. My dog is always eager for the journey. Through the rear view mirror, I see his nose pressed firmly against the back window, as if to count the telephone poles along the way. We are all conditioned to think that our lives revolve around great moments. However, great moments often catch us unaware, beautifully wrapped in small packages never easily forgotten. I sense the dog's joy, and we are silent riding together all the way.

> My soul finds rest in God alone; my
> salvation comes from him. He alone is my
> rock and my salvation; he is my fortress, I
> will never be shaken.

Psalm 62: 1, 2

MARCH 19, 2000

Over the years I have come to appreciate the word of encouragement. At age nine, I hung around a tennis club for one summer where the old Swedish pro, Johnny Larsen, came to know my name. He used to say, "Tom, you should practice more; you could be good at this." I blew it off as I did most things in those days and went about my business of doing nothing. Occasionally, I would see Johnny in passing and again hear his admonition, "Tom, you should spend more time on this; you might be good at it." I always sidestepped his words and walked away.

Then, one day my life at home became unbearable, and I did take the old tennis pro at his word, asking if he would really show me how to play. My dad refused to pay for tennis lessons; so, I asked Mr. Larsen if he would allow me to sit courtside while he taught those who "did" have the money to pay. I sat there in the grass, hour after hour, soaking in all the words and hundreds of ideas the pro spoke for the benefit of his students. That is how it all began. From that point on, I was there every day and every night, returning home late each evening, hoping always to arrive without stirring up the forces of hate that surrounded me there.

It was there, working in the tennis shop each afternoon with Johnny, that I learned the truth about the old pro. You see, the admonitions he had spoken to me about staying in the game, well, he spoke them, not just to "Tom" but to everyone. I thought his words had been directed *only* to me, and I came to fully believe them. The lesson I learned has never left me. Words falling from the tongue can be soft and mellow or they could be put to work as daggers, used to shred the listener into so many pieces. Consider your words wisely.... it was Mark Twain himself who observed "they are the difference between the lightning and the lightning bug."

> Reckless words pierce like a sword, but the
> tongue of the wise brings healing.

Proverbs 12: 18

APRIL 6, 2000

The first pedals of light bloomed and found their way through the opened blinds, announcing the arrival of another day. The nurses and staff on the maternity floor scurry down the narrow hallway and quietly push open the door where the baby has only now been born. He is a small, pale infant with damp, soft brown hair. Naming him after his father's father, they call him Thomas.

Now, so many years later, I often wonder what happened there in that room that steamy summer morning. If only I knew. Did they always NOT want me or was that something that happened over time? So often I have wondered what were the words spoken by those who peered down upon my face for the very first time. Surely they wanted me then, at the beginning, didn't they? I could have been guilty of nothing there, could have offended no one there, could have angered no one there. What happened to change all that? Did I commit the unforgivable act or represent the unforgivable past? I do not know. However, if the Creator of all Life wanted me, why did not the creators of my life?

> Before I formed you in the womb I knew
> you, before you were born I set you apart . .
>
> Jeremiah 1: 5

JUNE 14, 2000

While many may not be aware of it, in the early years of the Revolutionary War, Benedict Arnold was one of the colonial heroes for the American cause. It is quite a quirk of history that if a British bullet had ended his life early in the conflict, his name would have gone down as one of the bravest of the brave.

But, it did not happen that way. Instead, Arnold grew impatient with George Washington and the American Congress and went over to the British in the last years of the war. Because of one man's decision to betray his country, the name of "Benedict Arnold" will be forever synonymous with the word "traitor."

I bring up that story really for my own purposes. It reminds me how each decision we make in this life will not remain isolated from who we really are. For, looking back, our lives will be measured by each decision we settle on, and history will tend to know us by the ones we make late in life. It is now late in my own life, and I guard each step and consider every word so carefully. Those who will look back upon my time here hopefully will forgive the muddled days of my youth; but, rightly hold me accountable to the days I walked in the glory of the grace of the Lord our God.

> Therefore everyone who hears these words
> of mine and puts them into practice is like a
> wise man who built his house on the rock.

Matthew 7: 24

JUNE 29, 2000

Sara gave birth to her first child, Clay Daniel Black, late this day. I paced in the hallway outside the delivery room for twenty minutes before a sympathetic nurse poked her head out the door and announced, "He's here!" For a few moments, I was unable to speak or think rationally—a boy, a grandson, it is a joy beyond mere words. Before the birth, I had a few minutes alone with the new mom and wanted to give her a sense of the enormity about to take place. I thought back to Sara's own birth in 1976 and my driving anxiously to the hospital many years ago, knowing that after this day nothing would ever again be the same. For there, in the arrival of my own daughter, did I stumble upon a treasure of lessons that still reveal themselves to me. I am reminded once again of this wondrous experience that we call "life." May we hold close those whom the Lord has placed in our trust, knowing that one day death will separate us in the flesh. Confident that Sara and the newborn were doing well, I drove back across the Georgia line into Tennessee. In the car, I asked the Lord to allow me, having witnessed Clay's first birth, to live long enough to see his "second" also...his face to face meeting one day with the Prince of Peace.

> "How can a man be born when he is old?" Nicodemus asked. "Surely he cannot enter a second time into his mother's womb to be born!" Jesus answered, "I tell you the truth, no one can enter the kingdom of God unless he is born of water and the Spirit. Flesh gives birth to flesh, but the Spirit gives birth to spirit. You should not be surprised at my saying, 'You must be born again.'"
>
> John 3: 4, 5, 6, 7

JUNE 30, 2000

I awoke this morning at three a.m.
While I do not consider myself a prophet, I have a prophetic word that would not allow me to remain asleep until it was recorded here:

"For Scott and Sara: This day just passed will be one you shall never forget. Today you assume the most sacred responsibility ever placed in the humble hands of mortal men. As parents, you most certainly will be subjected to every emotional ebb and flow this wicked life can deliver. You both will now know joy unimaginable, and occasionally, sadness overwhelming. But, because of your son, neither of you will ever be the same again. From this moment forward, your lives are no longer your own, and your heirs will call you both "the wonderful ones." And your son, Clay, will be the firstborn of a new breed of men of our family, born a slave, not to alcohol, but a slave at the cross of Christ. Finally, you shall rejoice and hold close this gift of God for as long as you both shall live."

> They will not toil in vain or bear children
> doomed to misfortune; for they will be a
> people blessed by the Lord, they and their
> descendants with them. Before they call I
> will answer; while they are still speaking I
> will hear.

Isaiah 65: 23, 24

JULY 6, 2000

I drove down across the Georgia line tonight to see my grandson, Clay, at Hutcheson Memorial Hospital. He remains in the level II nursery, surrounded 24 hours a day by a terrific team of doctors and nurses. Scott and Sara were already there, and while Sara bottle-fed the baby, I read one of my favorites to him—Romans chapter eight. I knew full well the child, now only six days upon the earth, would sleep throughout my few minutes there. I read to him the words of life, "Therefore, there is now no condemnation for those who are in Christ Jesus," that majestic offering that instantly sets us all free.

Later that evening, as I drove back from the hospital in Fort Oglethorpe, the thunderstorm that had accompanied me down drifted away. Now, the drizzle slowed to a soft mist and lit up the horizon with a bright red hue. I could not help but sit back and see the moment in the full light of the years that had brought me to this place. I could easily have lost my life many years ago and not been here to witness the birth of my first grandson. It could have happened that way, but it did not. I am here; we are all here, alive and rich beyond all measure. I am very fortunate indeed. A man who has earned nothing, yet has been given everything; a man deserving of nothing, yet has been filled to overflowing.

> Jesus answered, "Everyone who drinks this water
> will be thirsty again, but whoever drinks the water
> I give him will never thirst. Indeed, the water I give
> him will become in him a spring of water welling
> up to eternal life."

John 4: 13, 14

JULY 11, 2000

My cocker spaniel, like myself, has grown old and feeble as time has rolled on. He is seventeen years old. Some have suggested that I should have him mercifully "put down," and often the idea is advanced that he has more than lived his life span. But God has decided to keep him around for a while as my companion. You see, I have laid hands on him and asked for his life to be continued, and the Lord has seen fit, for the time being, to grant my humble prayer. I just could not bear to see him go, and I am simply unable to say goodbye to such a friend as he.

In times past, when most of my "friends" decided not to remain with me, the old dog stayed constantly by my side. And when hearing that I was "not what people thought I should be," the old boy paid no attention and never strayed. So, now is the time when I shall begin to repay the debt. For no matter what may happen, I shall remain at his side.

I will never understand why the old dog, who never even knew my name, loved me unconditionally, while so many others, who knew my heart, could not love me at all.

> Love does not delight in evil but rejoices
> with the truth. It always protects, always
> trusts, always hopes, always perseveres.

I Corinthians 13: 6, 7

JULY 28, 2000

It was really a small squall that blew up late yesterday evening, but still the damage was great. A huge tree collapsed under the high winds and crushed the cab of my parked car. The policeman who appeared on the scene commented to me later that, luckily, I had "escaped death."

His remark bothered me for several days afterward. I mean, why would anyone even desire to "escape death?" Why would I put off for one instant that most glorious event of them all—that first moment of unspeakable joy, when I am face to face with the Lord of Lords? Why delay that split second in time and space when all my sorrows will be washed away, when all my uncertainty is lost in an endless sea of glory? Why put off that day.... when all the choirs of all the ages will serenade His name? A place where the angels of my heart will fly once more—why, oh why, would I want to "escape" this place?

> When the perishable has been clothed with the imperishable, and the mortal with immortality, then the saying that is written will come true: "Death has been swallowed up in victory."
>
> I Corinthians 15: 54

SEPTEMBER 19, 2000

My cocker spaniel's legs have begun to collapse below him. I am forced to confront the fact that his time is drawing to a close, and that my time to deal with his loss is also very near. So, for one last time, I carried him to the car and propped him up to see out the back window. Together we headed off down our favorite ride, along vine-draped Old Lee Highway turning at Apison Pike, crossing back to Ringgold Road and returning through Standifer Gap. We were both quite subdued, knowing surely that this would be our last journey together. Somewhat sickly, he strained every muscle to view the roadside passing by.

As fate would have it, the old dog collapsed and died late that afternoon of a heart attack. I cried so very much and could not stop. Sara came over with Scott late that evening, and together we decided that Pogo would be buried in the shade of the trees behind their home on Hunter Valley Road. I loved that dog. I have asked the Lord for a special gift—that Pogo should be there to meet me at the glorious gates into the Kingdom of Heaven.

> Martha said unto him, "I know that Lazarus
> shall rise again in the resurrection at the last day."
> Jesus said unto her, "I am the resurrection and
> the life: he that believeth in me, though he
> were dead, yet shall he live".
>
> John 11: 24, 25

OCTOBER 1, 2000

Pogo is now gone. No words I could record here would adequately describe my loss. It is now the silence that seeks to destroy me. No longer am I greeted with overwhelming joy at my mere arrival. I know I must keep my balance here and go about my life as usual, but I am suspended here in grief too deep to describe. At the depth of depression, he would come and sit at my side and allow me to cry, reminding me all over again how much he loved me. I never had a friend as loyal….for he asked no questions and passed no judgment of me. I will let him go, but I will never let him be forgotten.

Look around you, at those whom our merciful Lord has given you charge over. Remember, tomorrow they all may be gone. Love them now. Cherish with every fiber of your being all that has come your way, taking no one, no thing, and no event for granted.

The end of all things is near.

Therefore be clear minded and self-
controlled so that you can pray. Above all,
love each other deeply, because love covers
over a multitude of sins.

I Peter 4: 7, 8

NOVEMBER 22, 2000

Early in the morning of April 1, 1960, my father's life came to an end. The cause of death was later confirmed to be that of cirrhosis of the liver. But, in my eyes, daddy had left us many years earlier, forcing all who were his family to be eyewitnesses as he slipped further and further away into his own lonely existence. Each day he tortured us with his personality swings—loving, hating, and then loving us again without remorse. We needed him, but he chose, instead, to cherish his own voluntary madness. Sadly, I was a boy at his passing and so traumatized that I have no remembrance of the events that led up to his funeral or what followed. He was laid to rest in the family plot in northern Alabama, and now, 40 years later, I will return to the gravesite near the present town of Decatur.

NOVEMBER 23, 2000

I left Chattanooga in mid morning and crossed into Alabama around noon, arriving soon thereafter at the cemetery where much of my family rested. It was a cold, damp afternoon that saw me meandering among hundreds of marbled stones in search of the one bearing my father's name. But it was nowhere to be seen. That was the way it had always been for me since the beginning—my searching everywhere for daddy, but never being able to find him. I wandered aimlessly on the grounds before suddenly stumbling upon our name chiseled there in front of me. The familiarity of the words carved into the headstone froze me in place. I stood silently, staring at the ground for some time, thinking back to all those days when I had cried out for him only to watch as he turned and walked away. Thank God I am still alive, able to write the story of our lives from this moment forward.

All of us who are parents...we must seize the overwhelming import of our place in life—to care for those placed in our protection and leave them with the eternal message of hope. And when it is all over for us here, leave many fond memories behind. Let them remember how we held their hands when they were ill, and how we encouraged them when they were sad. Let them remember how we prayed God to keep them safe and held them close in times of trouble. Let them remember how we set aside our own ambitions to see their dreams come true. Let them remember that we loved without conditions and wept with them in moments of distress. Let them remember that we prayed for them and pointed them toward Jesus who is the Christ. Let them remember our love was always there, even when it seemed it was not. Let them remember those special times together, when we laughed and smiled and rejoiced in the happiness of life. Finally, let them sleep in peace, knowing that our separation is for but a season.

> For the Lord himself will come down from
> heaven, with a loud command, with the

voice of the archangel and with the trumpet call of God, and the dead in Christ will rise first. After that, we who are still alive and are left will be caught up together with them in the clouds to meet the Lord in the air. And so we will be with the Lord forever. Therefore encourage each other with these words.

I Thessalonians 4: 16, 17, 18

JANUARY 8, 2001

Recently, I went back to the house on Hunter Valley Road. There, at the edge of the clearing under the shady limb of an old tree, was Pogo's grave. I stood there, in a field of leaves, sharing with him some of my story since we had last been together. How I had known many days, some good some bad, but all would have been better had he been there as well. I promised him that there would be a day coming when we would walk together again, but that was not the first time I had shed tears over the grave of one of my dogs.

When I was just a boy, my first dog, Skippy, had been hit and killed one evening by a car near our home. Returning later that night, my sister had found him lying there crumpled by the side of the road. To prevent me from seeing the awful sight, she had taken his limp body up on the walkway over the bridge nearby and dropped him into the river below. When I learned what had happened, a heart broken little boy cried for what seemed an eternity as I had never gotten the chance to say goodbye to my best friend. So, the next day at first light, I mounted my bicycle and pedaled down to the bridge just hoping that I would see him one last time. I ran nervously across the span, back and forth, staring intensely down at the water crashing into the embankments below. But Skippy was no where to be found. I considered he must have sunk below the surface by now and was buried at sea. I had so much wanted to find him. I bicycled down to the far end of the bridge and suddenly saw the outline of a dog lying there motionless on the sandy shore. We sat there together at the water's edge for most of the afternoon with no words needing to be spoken. As the sun disappeared, I dug a deep hole there in the dirt with my hands and covered his broken torso so no one would ever see him again. I had stuck a small prayer book in my back pocket before leaving the house; so, I read some words committing him to the Lord before I pedaled away. When I left him there that day, I thought I would never see him again.

So we fix our eyes not on what is seen,
but on what is unseen.
For what is seen is temporary, but
what is unseen is eternal.

2 Corinthians 4: 18

MAY 30, 2002

Sara's second child, Riley, was born this day. I was working in North Carolina, so Scott called me with the glorious news. I could not help but cry just hearing his voice over the phone telling me of the arrival of another boy. Words cannot describe how happy I am. I began this life told that I would not long experience it and now I live to see my own grow strong and prosper. The Lord pours out on me more riches than I ever would have thought possible and I am humbled by the gifts which come my way. His love has redeemed us from both the hand of Pharaoh and the fist of all who would do us harm. The Lord is good.... His mercy is new every morning and His truth endures forever.

> You turned my wailing into dancing;
> you removed my sackcloth and
> and clothed me with joy, that my heart
> may sing to you and not be silent.
> O Lord my God, I will give you
> thanks forever.
>
> Psalm 30: 11, 12

SEPTEMBER 11, 2002

They were just young kids from the local junior college, out on their first date. It is rumored they were drinking in the car and did not notice the warning lights flashing up ahead. The speeding Honda sailed over the bulkhead and dove headfirst into the freezing pond, drowning both of them in the black watery night.

I sat there listening to the news report in stunned silence. Why will no one listen? How many friends will be lost; how many families destroyed; how many careers ruined? How many marriages will be dissolved; how many businesses will fail before we find our senses? How many children will not eat this night because their parents will not feed them? How many will die this day in the innocence of youth as they pay an eternal price for their own foolishness? How many of you will cast away my words as though I am a fool, only to recall them tomorrow when it is too late, in that last fleeting moment as the water slowly rises above *your* head?

> Choose my instruction instead of silver,
> knowledge rather than choice gold,
> for wisdom is more precious than rubies,
> and nothing you desire can compare with her.

Proverbs 8: 10, 11

NOVEMBER 30, 2002

I had made so many mistakes of both commission and omission in the raising of my daughter that I often stood in disbelief that we recovered from them all. Over the years she had become a wonderful, wonderful woman of faith....loved by her husband, admired by her friends, idolized by her children and adored by her father. Now I am convinced not *every* angel was sent to earth with wings. The Lord will bless whomever he chooses to bless and on this occasion he had opened the windows of heaven. I noted here words she sent me recently.....

Dear Dad, I just wanted you to know that I fully realize the price that you and Aunt Susan paid to give us, the future generations, a life free of generational curses. By accepting Christ and His gift of love, you both have passed on to us a great legacy. Because of the choices you have made, me, my children and my grandchildren will begin a new line in our family....people who know that, while life brings many difficulties, we have a greater hope in Jesus the completer of our faith. Thank you from the bottom of my heart for breaking the cycle of destruction and allowing all of us to live free in Christ. I love you....
Sara

Honor your father and your mother,
so that you may live long in the land
the Lord your God is giving you.

Exodus 20: 12

FEBRUARY 3, 2003

My life and my body are fast eroding, and I will soon be on the other shore. Weary am I of this world and wounded all over by years of surviving in it. For we do not perish at death….. we perish living everyday in a world corrupted at every seam where evil flourishes like the green of summer. In all my days upon the earth I can say that those animals placed in my care befriended me most. There was my boyhood dog, *Skippy,* who along with *Spencer* and *Little Boy*, were lost over the years under the wheels of passing cars. As well, I was forced to say goodbye to *Jip* and *Shepard* when our family separated in 1981, never seeing them again. Then there was *Alli Black,* who saved my life one night in Tennessee. And, of course, there was my floppy-eared cocker, *Pogo,* who trusted me when no one else would. I have pleaded with the Lord that these, who all loved me without conditions, should be the first to greet me at the doorway to the Kingdom of God. Oh what a day that will be.

And every evening, as soft breezes pass across my face, I will walk for endless hours, surrounded by this playful cadre of four-legged friends, through plush green meadows that rise and fall and never end. We are joyously together again. Now…there are only tears of laughter for finally, at last, I am home.

> Although the fig tree shall not blossom,
> neither shall fruit be in the vines;
> the labor of the olive shall fail,
> and the fields shall yield no meat;
> the flock shall be cut off from the fold,
> and there shall be no herd in the stalls;
> yet I will rejoice in the Lord, I will joy
> in the god of my salvation.

Habakkuk 3: 17, 18

APRIL 2, 2004

I have heard it said that the Lord our Father had made all things dependent on "faith"...so that whosoever has faith will have everything, and those without "faith" will go without. Well, I am not a theologian, and complex issues like this lead a simple man such as myself toward what I "do" know to be true, and that is this:

We have an invisible, immortal father, whose unfathomable love for us far exceeds all that we could ever imagine.

This is He who is a father to the father-less, a friend to the friendless, and He alone calls all the stars by name. This is He who banished all your gloom and sorrows, and made the sun to hide until the daybreak. This is He whose love for you is whispered in the morning's mist and echoed in the skylark's song. This is He who came to rescue the souls of men, sending us the holy ghost and saving us to the uttermost. This is He who taught me to climb so much steeper.... and love so much deeper.

This is He who lifted you when you could not stand and carried you when you could not walk. This is He who sang to you in the Autumn breeze and held your hand in the coldest night. This is He whose name is above all names and who, with His own hand, scribbled *your* name into the Book of Life. It is He alone who did these things, and we owe our allegiance to none other than He.

He is not like any other you have ever known, and once you have met Him, nothing will ever be the same again. When searching out the deepest stars in the darkest night, He is Elohim, the creator of all that ever was. When in need of a kind word, He is Jehovah Shalom, the Lord who is our peace. When ill, in need of the hand of the healer, He is Jehovah Rophe or perhaps Jehovah Jireh will come to you.

He is Elolam, the one who never changes, the First and the Last, the Bright and Morning Star. He is the Cornerstone, the Wonderful Counselor, Emmanuel, the King of Glory. He is the lamp, the song the shield. He is El Shaddai, the everlasting father, the author and the finisher of our faith. We are in love with Him and He with us. I am persuaded that our father knows neither ocean too wide nor valley too deep that He would not cross for us. And every evening, as night descends upon the city, he lights a candle and places it carefully on the window sill, knowing that we will soon be home.

> For it is we who are the circumcision,
> we who worship by the spirit of God,
> who glory in Christ Jesus,
> and who put no confidence in the flesh.
>
> Philippians 3: 3

JUNE 6, 2005

Many times I have stopped to consider how fortunate I was to have been born a citizen of a free nation such as this. A nation where the debate rages as to whether we are a "Christian" nation or merely a nation of Christians. Regardless, through my eyes, the men and women of the United States military, who guard that freedom overseas, are simply the best of the best! From the patriots at Bunker Hill to those who stood with Washington at Valley Forge to the heroes of this present day, they will always have my deepest respect. But I have always held a special place in my heart for that group of men who 61 years ago on this very date, landed and headed up the beach at Normandy on a mission to free occupied Europe. Many were gunned down before they even reached the shore by German gunners, perched in fortified positions set up high above the cliffs. That very evening, the President of the United States came to the nation by radio and spoke of these brave warriors and all those who would soon follow. His prayer on behalf of this nation is powerful and I note it here for your encouragement....

"Almighty God: our sons, pride of our nation, this day have set upon a mighty endeavor, a struggle to preserve our republic, our religion, and our civilization, and to set free a suffering humanity. Lead them straight and true; give strength to their arms, stoutness to their hearts, steadfastness in their faith. They will need Thy blessings. Their road will be long and hard. For the enemy is strong. He may hurl back our forces. Success may not come with rushing speed, but we shall return again and again; and we know that by Thy grace, and by the righteousness of our cause, our sons will triumph. They will be sore tried, by night and by day, without rest-until the victory is won. The darkness will be rent by noise and flame. Men's souls will be shaken with the violences of war. For these men are lately drawn from the ways of peace. They fight not for the lust of conquest. They fight to end conquest. They fight to liberate. They fight to let justice arise, and tolerance and goodwill among all Thy people. They yearn for the end of battle, for the return to the haven of home. Some will never return. Embrace them, Father, and receive them, Thy heroic servants into Thy Kingdom. And for us at home- fathers, mothers, children, wives, sisters and brothers of brave men overseas, whose thoughts and prayers are ever with them- help us, Almighty God, to rededicate ourselves in renewed faith in thee in this hour of great sacrifice. Many people have urged that I call the nation into a single day of special prayer. But because the road is long and the desire is great, I ask that our people devote themselves in a continuance of prayer. As we rise to each new day, and again when each day is spent, let words of prayer be on our lips, invoking Thy help to our efforts. Give us strength, too- strength in our daily tasks, to redouble the contributions we make in the physical and material support of our armed forces. And let our hearts be stout, to wait out the long travail, to bear sorrows that may come, to impart courage unto our sons wheresoever they may be. And, O Lord, give us faith. Give us faith in thee; faith in our sons; faith in each other, faith in our united crusade. Let not the keenness of our spirit ever be dulled. Let not the impacts of temporary events, of temporal matters of but fleeting moments- let not these deter us in our unconquerable purpose. With Thy blessing, we shall prevail over the unholy forces of our enemy. Help us to conquer the apostles of greed and racial arrogances. Lead us to the saving of our country, and with our sister nations into a world unity that will spell a sure peace- a peace invulnerable to the schemings of unworthy men. And a peace that will let all men live in freedom, reaping the just reward of their honest toil. Thy will be done, Almighty God, Amen".

Franklin Delano Roosevelt
President of the United States
June 6, 1944

AUGUST 9, 2006

Some who viewed the early draft of this manuscript have asked why I even bothered to record these words over all these years. "Let bygones be bygones" I often heard. The answer of course is layered in too complex a ball of yarn for someone as simple as me to unwind. Like most of you, I desired my life to have been spent for good and if I can reach out with the promise of hope, then the price I have paid will have been well worth the journey. These then are my love letters, sent to those who, every morning, laid down their lives for me. I believe and I know that I do not stand alone on the bold principle of God, Country, Family and that this wonderful land has been blessed with many who share those same ideals.

One of those was a family friend, "Uncle Gene", who died many years ago and yet whose memory still resides in the warmest part of my heart. He had called me several weeks before my first days as a college student and insisted I spend one morning with him alone. We went to the heart of the business district and entered the well known and very expensive men's store which occupied an entire city block. Uncle Gene knew full well that I had no money and he proceeded to spend hundreds of his own dollars to insure that I would be well dressed throughout my first year in university. I was young and very selfish in those days and my "Thank you" as we parted was surely not enough. I did not see Gene again until one day, many years later, I stumbled into a large church in the downtown area and was asked to sit in the balcony as the early arrivals had filled up the seats below. Within minutes I spotted Uncle Gene far below me on the ground floor, his hands waving and feet dancing in celebration of the gospel of Christ. At that moment it all began to come together for me. Only then did I come to understand that the men who served the Lord were also servants to the poor, the lost, the weak and the lame. And it was because I was *all* of those, that Uncle Gene had emptied his wallet that day on my behalf. So I now write to all who have ears to hear…"Silver and gold have I none; but such as I have I give thee; in the name of Jesus Christ of Nazareth, rise up and walk."

> For I was hungry and you gave me something to eat,
> I was thirsty and you gave me something to drink,
> I was a stranger and you invited me in,
> I needed clothes and you clothed me,
> I was sick and you looked after me,
> I was in prison and you came to visit me……
> The King will reply, "I tell you the truth, whatever you
> did for one of the least of these brothers of mine,
> you did it for me."

Matthew 25: 35, 36, 40

FEBRUARY 2, 2007

It is apparent to me now that all of us struggle with the issue of our own self-worth. Every morning we stare into the mirror and question the value of that person we see there in front of us.

Over the years I have crossed the path of many who sought to inflate their self esteem through acts of great charity and human kindness. Others have been driven to athletic heights and found themselves praised and adored by all. And still some poor souls have given up much too soon, succumbing to the lure of drugs, allowing their bodies to fall to a slow but certain death.

I am only sad that it has taken me so long to finally come upon the Truth. For completeness will *not* be found in *this* place or *that* place. It is found by finding *your* place in the heart of the majestic Son of God.

> Jesus answered, "I am the Way and the Truth
> and the Life. No one comes to the Father
> except through me."
>
> John 14: 6

NOVEMBER 9, 2007

Hallelujah, our family grew by one today. Sara and Scott had their third child, a little girl, Emmi, and we all were moved to tears by the wonder of it all. A grandfather now for the third time, I declare a season of child spoiling and I appoint myself as an ambassador of one to see that it is done. As a small boy I had stared up at the ceiling many nights wondering if I would live to see the next dawn. Now, after so much time has passed, I stand amazed at what the days have brought. Our family is well and we are watched over day and night by the angels of the Lord. He has presided over the liberation of our lives, the increase of our numbers and the linking together of our hearts. His hand has steadied our days and His eyes have guided us through the maze and confusion of this life. The words have never been written that would allow us to say how grateful we are. So we go forth from this day proclaiming to all who will listen that the Messiah *has* come! And like the apostle, I consider everything a loss compared to the surpassing greatness of knowing the Christ, for whose sake I have lost all things.

> "The Spirit of the Lord is upon me, because He hath anointed me to preach the gospel to the poor; He hath sent me to heal the brokenhearted, to preach deliverance to the captives, and recovering of sight to the blind, to set at liberty them that are bruised, to preach the acceptable year of the Lord." And He closed the book, and He gave it again to the minister, and sat down. And the eyes of all them that were in the synagogue were fastened on Him. And He began to say unto them, "This day is the scripture fulfilled in your ears."

Luke 4: 18, 19, 20, 21

DECEMBER 23, 2007

Oh Father, how deep is your love for me? Poets cannot find the words, writers unable to write it, singers unable to sing it. I spend moonlit nights perched alone below the willow tree, confounded by it all. For now, with the coming of the carpenter, Love Everlasting finally has a name.

You ask, "How much does He love me"......how deep is the ocean, how high is the sky? It is beyond the understanding of mortal men to lay hold to such a treasure, placed so freely into the hearts of those who are not ashamed of the gospel of Jesus Christ. Perhaps it means so much more to me now, reflecting back to those days when *love* was merely a simple word. For He was with me, even before I knew His name.

In Exodus, He is *The Passover Lamb*, in Joshua, *The Captain of our Salvation*, in Revelation, *The Lion of the Tribe of Judah*. And to me, this is He who stood at my bedside each night, when I was a small child, and whose hand shielded me from certain harm. Yea, though I walk through the valley of the shadow of death, I will fear no evil, for thou art with me. What other King would have left His throne for me?

Oh Father, dearest Father, my words are so lacking to speak what love is in my heart for my Deliverer. When no one would take my hand, You gave me Yours. It is like a beggar, without shoes, sad and hungry, who is suddenly asked to share the riches of his King. But I am not alone.

He has come for all of us...the meek and the bold, the slave and the free....for all who will call upon His name.

His mercy survives all wars, rises above all conflicts, soars above all kings. He lifts us in the storm, follows us in the night, surrounds us in the morn. No forest can hide you, no trail will guide you to that place where His love is not already there. He is behind me, beside me, and always before me. His presence is everlasting to everlasting and, of His kingdom, there shall be no end. And I shall live all my days declaring

His name to be the One whom the prophets revealed. For He has come, yes, He that liveth and was dead, and behold is alive for evermore.

> I cease not to give thanks for you, making mention of you in my prayers; that the God of our Lord Jesus Christ, the Father of glory, may give unto you the spirit of wisdom and revelation in the knowledge of Him
>
> Ephesians 1: 16, 17

DECEMBER 24, 2007

Sand is flowing out of the hourglass and there can be no doubt that I am a flower quickly fading. I need to say goodbye to so many, but there is so little time. My hope is that all of you who will read these words will find the path to which you have been called rather than the one of least resistance. As the minutes pass into hours, be reminded that the unconditional love your heart so desires begins and ends in the Kingdom of the Most High God. Remember always that it was His hand that carved out the valleys that you walk through.....for you will never realize that Jesus is all you need.....until the day arrives when Jesus is all you have. Be reminded that you are adored in heavenly places and that the face of our Father lights up at the very mention of your name.

Lastly, to my daughter, Sara, I would leave her with these thoughts:

Oh my darling, you have made my days so sweet that I have no words left to tell you how much I love you. I will always recall those days when you and I were both so young and life was all so new. You will never know how honored I have been that the Creator of all things would have chosen me from the beginning of time to have been in this place for you. You have given meaning to my life that no one will ever be able to take away. I was there at your very first day of school and held your arm as we walked joyously down the aisle. You enriched my every moment, and the recollection of those days is a treasure I will take with me always. In giving you to me, the Father expressed His glorious love and mercy, that someone as flawed as I, should receive such a precious gift. On the landscape of my life, colored in with so many browns and grays, you have always been my rainbow. So sleep well my love, fearing nothing; for I have passed from death unto life.

I will always love you...
Daddy

I saw the Holy City, the new Jerusalem, coming down out of heaven from God, prepared as a bride beautifully dressed for her husband. And I heard a loud voice from the throne saying, "Now the dwelling of God is with men, and he will live with them. They will be his people, and God himself will be with them and be their God. He will wipe every tear from their eyes.

There will be no more death or mourning or crying or pain, for the old order of things has passed away."

Revelation 21: 2, 3, 4

We ask that you *not* keep this book after having read it. Instead, the author would have you give it away. Send it to a friend, to a roommate or perhaps a son or daughter on their way to college. The manuscript was never intended to be locked away or hidden away on a library shelf. May the Lord bless and keep you. The Lord make His face to shine upon you, and be gracious unto you; The Lord lift up His countenance upon you and give you peace.

>Thomas Lile
>Chattanooga, Tennessee
>January/2008
>Email: tommylile@hotmail.com

And ye shall be witnesses unto me both in Jerusalem, and in all Judea, and in Samaria, and unto the uttermost part of the earth.

Acts 1: 8

REFERENCES

Barker, Kenneth, ed. The NIV Study Bible. Grand Rapids: Zondervan Publishing House, 1985.

Bennett, William J. Our Sacred Honor. New York: Simon and Schuster, 1997.

Irving, Washington. George Washington: A Biography. New York: DACAPO Press, 1994.

Twain, Mark. The Art of Authorship. Ed.- George Bainton: New York: Appleton, 1890

Made in the USA
Charleston, SC
20 April 2012